Component-Based
Development

The Addison-Wesley Object Technology Series

Grady Booch, Ivar Jacobson, and James Rumbaugh, Series Editors

For more information check out the series web site [http://www.aw.com/cseng/otseries/].

Armour/Miller, *Advanced Use Case Modeling, Volume 1*

Atkinson, *Component-based Product Line Engineering with UML*

Binder, *Testing Object-Oriented Systems: Models, Patterns, and Tools*

Blakely, *CORBA Security: An Introduction to Safe Computing with Objects*

Booch, *Object Solutions: Managing the Object-Oriented Project*

Booch, *Object-Oriented Analysis and Design with Applications, Second Edition*

Booch/Rumbaugh/Jacobson, *The Unified Modeling Language User Guide*

Box, *Essential COM*

Box/Brown/Ewald/Sells, *Effective COM: 50 Ways to Improve Your COM and MTS-based Applications*

Cockburn, *Surviving Object-Oriented Projects: A Manager's Guide*

Collins, *Design Object-Oriented User Interfaces*

Conallen, *Building Web Applications with UML*

D'Souza/Wills, *Objects, Components, and Frameworks with UML-The Catalysis Approach*

Douglass, *Doing Hard Time: Developing Real-Time Systems with UML: Objects, Frameworks, and Patterns*

Douglass, *Real-Time UML, Second Edition: Developing Efficient Objects for Embedded Systems*

Fontura/Pree/Rumpe, *The UML Profile for Framework Architectures*

Fowler, *Analysis Patterns: Reusable Object Models*

Fowler/Beck/Brant/Opdyke/Roberts, *Refactoring: Improving the Design of Existing Code*

Fowler/Scott, *UML Distilled, Second Edition: A Brief Guide to the Standard Object Modeling Language*

Gomaa, *Designing Concurrent, Distributed, and Real-Time Applications with UML*

Gorton, *Enterprise Transaction Processing Systems: Putting the CORBA OTS, Encina++ and Orbix OTM to Work*

Heinckiens, *Building Scalable Database Applications: Object-Oriented Design, Architectures, and Implementations*

Hofmeister/Nord/Dilip, *Applied Software Architecture*

Jacobson/Booch/Rumbaugh, *The Unified Software Development Process*

Jacobson/Christerson/Jonsson/Overgaard, *Object-Oriented Software Engineering: A Use Case Driven Approach*

Jacobson/Ericsson/Jacobson, *The Object Advantage: Business Process Reengineering with Object Technology*

Jacobson/Griss/Jonsson, *Software Reuse: Architecture Process and Organization for Business Success*

Jordan, *C++ Object Databases: Programming with the ODMG Standard*

Kruchten, *The Rational Unified Process, An Introduction, Second Edition*

Lau, *The Art of Objects: Objects-Oriented Design and Architecture*

Leffingwell/Widrig, *Managing Software Requirements: A Unified Approach*

Marshall, *Enterprise Modeling with UML: Designing Successful Software through Business Analysis*

Mowbray/Ruh, *Inside CORBA: Distributed Object Standards and Applications*

Oestereich, *Developing Software with UML: Object-Oriented Analysis and Design in Practice*

Page-Jones, *Fundamentals of Object-Oriented Design in UML*

Pohl, *Object-Oriented Programming Using C++, Second Edition*

Pooley/Stevens, *Using UML: Software Engineering with Objects and Components*

Quatrani, *Visual Modeling with Rational Rose 2000 and UML*

Rector/Sells, *ATL Internals*

Reed, *Developing Applications with Visual Basic and UML*

Rosenberg/Scott, *Use Case Driven Object Modeling with UML: A Practical Approach*

Royce, *Software Project Management: A Unified Framework*

Ruh/Herron/Klinker, *IIOP Complete: Understanding CORBA and Middleware Interoperability*

Rumbaugh/Jacobson/Booch, *The Unified Modeling Language Reference Manual*

Schneider/Winters, *Applying Use Cases: A Practical Guide*

Shan/Earle, *Enterprise Computing with Objects: From Client/Server Environments to the Internet*

Warmer/Kleppe, *The Object Constraint Language: Precise Modeling with UML*

White, *Software Configuration Management Strategies and Rational ClearCase: A Practical Introduction*

Component Software Series

Clements Szyperski, Series Editor

Allen, *Realizing eBusiness with Components*

Cheesman/Daniels, *UML Components: A Simple Process for Specifying Component-based Software*

Component-Based Development:

Principles and Planning for Business Systems

KATHARINE WHITEHEAD

 **Addison-Wesley**

an imprint of **Pearson Education**

London ■ Boston ■ Indianapolis ■ New York ■ Mexico City ■ Toronto ■ Sydney ■ Tokyo ■ Singapore
Hong Kong ■ Cape Town ■ New Delhi ■ Madrid ■ Paris ■ Amsterdam ■ Munich ■ Milan ■ Stockholm

PEARSON EDUCATION LIMITED

Head Office:
Edinburgh Gate
Harlow CM20 2JE
Tel: +44 (0)1279 623623
Fax: +44 (0)1279 431059

London Office:
128 Long Acre
London WC2E 9AN
Tel: +44 (0)20 7447 2000
Fax: +44 (0)20 7240 5771

Website: www.it-minds.com
          www.aw.com/cseng/

First published in Great Britain in 2002

© Pearson Education Ltd 2002

The right of Katharine Whitehead to be identified as the Author of this Work has been asserted by her in accordance with the Copyright, Designs and Patents Act 1988.

ISBN 0-201-67528-5

British Library Cataloguing in Publication Data
A CIP catalogue record for this book can be obtained from the British Library

Library of Congress Cataloging in Publication Data
Whitehead, Katharine, 1958–
    Component-based development principles and planning for business systems /
Katharine Whitehead.
       p. cm. – (Component software series)
    Includes bibliographical references and index.
    ISBN 0-201-67528-5 (pbk.)
    1. Component software. 2. Application software–Development. 3. Management
information systems. I. Title. II. Series.

QA76.76.C66 W455 2002
005.3–dc21

                                                                              2002019835

10 9 8 7 6 5 4 3 2 1

Typeset by Mathematical Composition Setters Ltd, Salisbury, Wiltshire
Printed and bound in Great Britain by Biddles Ltd of Guildford and King's Lynn

The Publishers' policy is to use paper manufactured from sustainable forests.

Contents

Preface

This book tries to answer the questions: *What is it that we are trying to achieve with components?* and *How can we define and implement components so that we do achieve this?* It is intended to provide an insight into the specific benefits of component-based development (CBD) and to convey the conceptual issues that must be fully understood in order to be successful with CBD.

It aims to:

- explain the rationale for CBD and the key concepts behind it;
- outline an approach to program planning that should significantly improve the effectiveness of CBD;
- provide guidance on introducing a component-based approach into the organization;
- provide an understanding of the issues involved in the design and assembly of components, including strategies for scoping components and for managing their assembly.

It is left to other books in the field to provide technical insights into J2EE, .NET, etc. or to provide a full method that would necessarily have a heavy emphasis on modeling techniques. Instead, it is assumed that you will use a model-based development method (preferably OO or at least hybrid). This assumption makes it possible to concentrate in this book on issues that are specific to adopting a component-based approach, rather than discussing software development techniques that are already widely understood.

CBD is usually regarded as principally relevant to new software development. However, software development cannot take place in a vacuum. It must take account of the current application portfolio and existing software infrastructure of the organization. It is for this reason that this book pays particular attention to program planning. In this book, CBD and integration with existing systems are seen as natural partners. Software development is seen as a process of gradual migration forwards from an existing application portfolio to an improved (and more component-based) application portfolio. CBD provides a means of achieving this gradual improvement, while a component-based "vision" of how the application portfolio could ultimately look provides guidance as to how to move it forwards.

Audience

This book aims to meet the needs of practitioners, and in particular the needs of program planners and architects, who are likely to be responsible for achieving the introduction of CBD into the organization. Managers, designers, and developers should also find it of use.

Content and organization

The book contains the following parts and chapters.

PART 1   Introduction to component-based development

Chapter 1   Component-based development: attempting to managing chaos

This chapter explains the industry context within which CBD has emerged, and why CBD provides a way of dealing with the conflicting pressures facing software developers.

Chapter 2   What are components?

This chapter provides a definition of components and a discussion of component characteristics. It also discusses the environment required to support components, and briefly outlines the advantages and disadvantages of existing component models such as COM, CORBA, and EJB.

Chapter 3   Putting components in perspective

CBD is only a part of what is relevant for effective software development. This chapter positions CBD in relation to other development techniques, and in relation to OO. It also discusses the limitations to the potential of CBD, and the contexts in which it will not be relevant.

PART 2   The planning process

Chapter 4   Positioning components within the organization

This chapter discusses the ownership and scope of a CBD initiative and its positioning within the organization.

Chapter 5   Software architecture and infrastructure

This chapter discusses the need for an architecture and the various aspects that an architecture for CBD needs to cover.

Chapter 6   Defining components

This chapter covers the principles affecting component definition:

● coarse- versus fine-grained components;
● types of component and how they can be fitted together;
● defining component scope.

Emerging standards are discussed.

Chapter 7   Putting component-based development into practice

This chapter builds on the previous three chapters and outlines a set of tasks that can be carried out to create an initial CBD strategy and to refine this strategy over time.

Chapter 8   Pragmatics of program planning

This chapter discusses how the CBD strategy can be put into effect over time, as part of program planning. It covers the process of reconciling an ideal vision with short-term requirements and messy reality.

Chapter 9   Organization for component-based development

This chapter discusses alternative organizational structures for implementing a CBD program. It discusses roles and team structures for strategy planning, component acquisition, and component assembly.

PART 3   Building and assembling components

Chapter 10   Acquiring components

This chapter covers issues that are specific to procuring components as opposed to packages.

Chapter 11   Designing components

This chapter discusses how to design components for flexibility – and where to draw the line in designing for reuse.

Chapter 12   Assembling components

This chapter discusses some of the issues that arise when fitting components together.

Chapter 13   Testing, certification, and maintaining a component catalog

This chapter outlines issues relating to the management and maintenance of a portfolio of components, including a consideration of what is needed to make a component available for reuse or sale.

PART 4   A brief case study

Chapter 14   Managing chaos with components

This chapter contains a brief (fictional) case study of the use of CBD in an organization with existing mainframe-based applications that is evolving toward a component-based approach, as it introduces call centers and Internet-based systems.

Acknowledgments

The origins of this book lie in work on components that my colleagues and I carried out while I was working at Seer Technologies. I owe much to Jon Cogdale, who was my collaborator on our original research into components, and my examples in Chapter 7 are based on his. Graham Berrisford contributed lively and thought-provoking discussion of the concepts, and the order processing examples in Chapter 12 owe much to discussions with him. Amongst my colleagues, Doug Kime, Rob Allen, Tony Phillips, Bernard Londeix, Mark Gilbert, and Martin Carter also offered valuable advice.

I also learned from the experiences our customers shared with us, from the CBDi Forum run by David Sprott and Lawrence Wilkes, as well as from other literature and work in the field.

Introduction to component-based development

Component-based development: attempting to manage chaos

The objective of CBD is to improve the software development process by assembling new software from pre-built software components rather than developing it from scratch.

Why should this be desirable? To answer this question, let us consider some of the problems that we have experienced with software development over the past 20 years or more.

1.1 Problems of software development

1.1.1 Software is difficult to maintain

In the first place, software is hard to maintain. It seems as if the ramifications of every change we make spread their tentacles far and wide within each system we deploy. We have to delve into large amounts of code in order to determine whether changes can be made safely and what code needs to change.

Of course, code is not usually well documented. And even if there is documentation, we cannot trust it to be up to date. As a result, only the code itself provides reliable documentation. Unfortunately, the code is usually not easy to understand. Code has its own inherent complexity that cannot be eliminated. Code is necessarily longwinded because everything has to be stated exactly if the computer is to follow the instructions, whereas in natural language communications we can leave gaps and hope that the human recipient of the communication will fill those gaps. Ideally, a programing language would enable us to express only the business logic, without other extraneous detail. Instead, the key logic of the application is swathed in code that is there for technical reasons – required in order to deal with the small vocabulary of the programing language, translate between data types, and so on. While this situation may improve, there is little reason to suppose that code will soon become easy to understand.

The difficulty of understanding code would matter less if the impact of a change could be localized, reducing the amount of code to be looked at, but it is usually difficult to draw a line around areas that might be impacted and those that will not. Much code must be inspected simply to check that it is not affected.

As a result, changes take a long time to achieve. This is a problem when business practices change so rapidly and the competitiveness of our business depends on our being able to adapt our business systems to new ways of doing business – at least as fast as the competition, and preferably faster.

1.1.2   The need for application integration

1.1.2.1   Changes in business practices

A second issue arises because we often develop applications in isolation and subsequently find that those applications must be integrated with each other.

It is obviously a practical approach to build applications independently. Decision making is easier when one department can decide to build the application it needs without involving the organization as a whole. Building a new, fully integrated solution to a company's software requirements is an organizational nightmare that organizations have never, to my knowledge, been foolish enough to attempt. Where very large-scale applications have been built from scratch, rather than accumulating over a period of time, these have been very high-risk projects that have had a high failure rate.

In fact, building independent applications with simple interfaces that, for instance, allow summary details from one application to be fed into a management information system, has been a very successful approach. However, it is an approach that breaks down when changes in the way business is done cause changes to the departmental boundaries that define the scope of our existing applications.

For example, a typical financial services company will have different applications to handle different types of business, such as:

● mortgages

● share plans (each type of share plan may be handled by a different application)

● insurance.

Similarly, a magazine publishing company will have different applications to deal with subscriptions, dispatch, and billing.

These different applications were typically specific to the needs of a single department. In the days when most business was transacted by post, this worked reasonably well. Many shortcomings could be covered up by using manual procedures. When we moved to handling most business transactions over the telephone, however, these shortcomings became difficult to mask.

For instance, when I change my address, I want to provide only one notification of my change of address to a company I have dealings with, not one to each department I deal with. And when I phone a company, I expect them to be able to deal with my questions on the spot. This implies at least that all the relevant applications must be available – and quickly – to the person on the other end of the phone. Really, to make information relevant to one customer available quickly, the whole organization of the navigation of the application needs to change so that all information related to one customer, rather than all information relevant to one department, is gathered by the user interface.

This has led to the requirement to integrate what have sometimes been called "stovepipe" applications – applications that reflect the departmental structure of the time at which they were built.

Indeed, in response to the increased focus on customers, many companies have also changed their organizational structure. Whereas previously they might have had one department for each type of financial instrument, they may now have departments that specialize in different types of customer, for instance corporate customers or individuals.

Figure 1.1 shows a schematic view of the nature of this type of change in the requirements placed on application structure. The figure shows the original

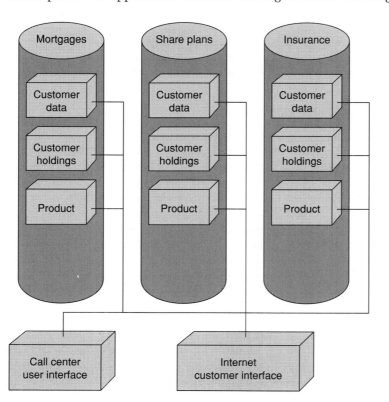

Figure 1.1
Integrating existing stovepipe applications

stovepipe applications for mortgages, share plans, and insurance that were built to meet the needs of individual departments within the organization. Two new applications are also shown, one for use by a call center and one for use by customers accessing information about their holdings over the Internet. These applications must gather information that is already managed by the separate stovepipe applications, and present it using a new user interface that groups all information relevant to each customer.

Unfortunately the original application structure of the "stovepipe" applications does not easily accommodate these changes in requirements. Often, the best solution in terms of quality would be to develop a new application, but this costs time and effort. It also leads to duplication of code between the new and old applications, with all the attendant maintenance issues involved in keeping duplicate code consistent. Usually, a way must be found to integrate the original applications in the short term, with some level of redevelopment being inevitable. Many of us in the software business, having experienced this type of problem, have become keen to find a way of developing any new applications we require so that they will not be similarly inflexible when the next round of changes is required.

Indeed, the current process of structural change in how our applications should be organized does not appear to have finished yet. On the contrary, the movement to e-commerce and e-business is resulting in further requirements for restructuring of applications, as well as further reorganization of businesses.

While it may be utopian to imagine there is a way of building applications that completely futureproofs them against this type of unanticipated change, it seems reasonable to suppose that some potential for improvement exists.

1.1.2.2   *Mergers and takeovers*

There are other business reasons that also lead to a requirement for application integration. The need arises as soon as two companies merge, or one is taken over. Where possible, the most economic approach is often to adopt the application portfolio of just one of the two merged organizations. However, wherever the two businesses do not completely overlap, so that applications from both companies are needed, it is likely that applications that were never expected to have to interoperate will need to be made to do so. There will inevitably be duplication of functionality between these applications. Customer details, in particular, will have been maintained by both merged companies, and will have been maintained differently. How are these to be merged?

The problems that arise are similar to those already discussed in the previous section.

1.1.2.3   *Packages*

The same issues arise wherever packaged applications are used. The functionality of a package will inevitably overlap with a company's in-house applications. And where more than one package is bought, these will overlap. The applications will require integration, but packaged applications are unlikely (at this point in time) to have been built in a way that facilitates this.

1.1.2.4 Start-ups

A start-up company cannot usually afford to start by building custom applications for use in-house. Instead, packaged applications must be used as far as possible. These are therefore likely to require integration.

At first, manual procedures are usually adopted to work around the lack of integration. But the same drivers that are currently prompting companies to integrate and restructure their in-house applications mean that better integration between applications is required by start-ups as well if they are to be competitive.

1.1.3 Presentation changes

In addition to these business-related issues, as the software industry has evolved, new requirements relating to the presentation of information have arisen. From the days of batch, before the use of visual display units was widespread, we have evolved through green screens to graphical user interfaces (GUI) and onwards to browser-based interfaces. Other forms of interface, such as e-mail or voice recognition, or scanning of documents, are also increasingly relevant.

Each time we have to present information differently, the question arises: *Can I simply bolt on a new front end to my existing application, or must I rewrite?* Usually, a rewrite is necessary. Generally, the application has not been written such that it has a detachable front end. User interface logic and business logic are inextricably mingled. Moreover, the sequence in which information should be presented in the new application is often different.

It is tantalising that delivery of what is, at least superficially, the same function – transferring money between accounts, for instance – requires a new application to handle each new delivery mechanism, e.g. a transfer at a bank through a bank clerk, a transfer requested over the phone (which may be received by a human operator or handled electronically), a transfer received by e-mail, a transfer request processed through the bank's web site, etc.

The need for alternative delivery mechanisms pushes in the direction of separating business logic and user interface logic, so that the common business logic can be reused.

1.1.4 Technology changes

Another frustrating factor is the speed at which technology changes. Sometimes it seems as if no sooner has software been developed using one technology than a new approach is preferred. This is undoubtedly partly due to the technical bias of those working in the field, who tend to favor the new and to be motivated by an intellectual curiosity that makes the newest idea seem like the best! It is also due to the fact that the field of software development is new, and consequently techniques and approaches are developing fast. Whatever the cause, the speed of technological change is a challenge that seems to threaten the longevity of each new development we undertake, however we undertake it.

1.1.5 Reimplementing the wheel

Software houses in particular find themselves in the position of developing similar applications for a number of customers. But even when a software house has just developed a warehousing application and found a new customer who also wants a warehousing application, the odds are that it will not be possible to reuse the previous application.

The most basic reason for this is that software is used to support processes that diverge naturally because different organizations simply achieve a similar external result in a different way. And people are likely to protect the divergences not just where they give genuine competitive advantage but also because people simply prefer to do things their own way – a pretty natural human characteristic that managers are ill-advised to ignore.

Even beyond these differences in requirements, developing software is essentially a creative activity. There is no single right solution, and consequently each individual architect or team naturally devises a solution that is structurally different from any other solution.

In spite of all these reasons for divergence, it is very much in a software house's interest to find a way of capitalizing on experience so that the cost of producing a solution can be decreased. In many cases, software houses can adapt a previously built application to a new customer's needs. Where a genuinely common solution can be developed, a product may emerge that can be sold as such. This is easiest in business areas that are relatively stable, such as accounting.

The challenge for the software house is to find a way of developing software so that previous solutions can be reused, and tailored to a new customer's specific requirements.

1.2 Steps toward improving software development

The previous section outlined some of the problems experienced with software development that CBD can help with, as we will explain shortly.

Obviously, CBD is just one of many attempts made over the years to improve the efficiency of software development. Previous attempts have had some success in addressing some of the issues outlined above, and indeed, CBD is not a complete departure from these attempts – instead it capitalizes on them.

This section outlines some of the previous attempts at improving the efficiency of software development.

1.2.1   Productivity tools

While now unfashionable, CASE (computer-aided software engineering) tools and 4GLs were the result of important initiatives to improve development productivity. CASE tools and 4GLs do not directly address the issues of application integration. They can be seen mainly as an attempt to address the issue of maintainability by reducing the complexity of code and improving its associated documentation.

The objective of a 4GL is to find a higher level of abstraction than that of a third-generation programing language so that programs can be written more quickly. 4GLs aim to achieve productivity improvements over third-generation programing languages just as third-generation programing languages achieved productivity improvements over assembly languages.

CASE tools, on the other hand, usually aim to offer assistance during the earlier stages in the project life cycle, such as analysis. CASE tools often become like 4GLs, however, at the point at which the transition from design into developing code occurs. At this point, they offer translation from what is effectively the CASE tool's own 4GL (acknowledged as such or not) into a third-generation programing language.

Generally, the fate of 4GLs has been to provide short-term benefits in areas requiring new development expertise – currently internet-related logic – but then to be superseded as any new elements required are absorbed back into mainstream languages and development environments.

Some of the development techniques of CASE and 4GL environments become adopted in development environments that enable the production of 3GL code. For instance, tools such as VisualAge have incorporated the use of so-called "visual programing" with diagrams and drag and drop.

While incorporating such ease-of-use capabilities into a 3GL development environment does improve programer productivity, particularly on first development of the code, it does not change the level of complexity of the code that is produced. This means that software maintenance remains difficult – locating all the code that has to be changed to fix a particular problem is as difficult as ever.

CASE tools and 4GLs, on their side, have suffered from a number of weaknesses, some of which are outlined below. Despite these weaknesses, there is no doubt that CASE tools and 4GLs have important potential, particularly if the most significant drawback – the lack of plug and play – can be addressed.

1.2.1.1   Level of abstraction of 4GLs

The objective of a 4GL is to move up from the level of a third-generation programing language. The next level of abstraction has, however, proved elusive.

What set of language constructs makes sense when moving beyond the set used in a 3GL? In order to make it possible to use fewer instructions to achieve a given result, presumably a larger number of less general-purpose constructs is needed. However, which should these be? Introducing business-level constructs is one approach, but this makes the vocabulary large and one on which there is little agreement.

Another approach is to use code frameworks and generate code into these frameworks.

Frameworks are prefabricated software that provide a partial solution for a family of related problems. A framework predefines the main data and control flow infrastructure of an application. The implementation is usually incomplete and is extended and customized by application builders to deliver a specific solution. A code framework supplies predefined code that is used in each resulting application without alteration, with the optional addition of template code that may be completed by filling the blanks, either by adding lines of code or by giving values to parameters. Whereas subroutines are reusable code invoked from an application, a framework is reusable code that generally invokes (or is alternatively inherited by) application-specific code. Frameworks are an approach that can be used both for object-oriented (OO) and other code.

Frameworks may be visible, with their code available for inspection. They may be provided as programing artefacts (e.g. sets of programing templates), or they may be packaged into application builders, in which a development tool assists you in inserting code into relevant parts of the framework, such as event handlers and triggers.

Basically, the approach works by formalizing a standard application architecture, and adopting standard design patterns within that architecture, and then fitting each application into this standard architecture. In most cases, only a part of the architecture is standardized. For instance, the handling of the user interface has been a common candidate for standardization and the use of frameworks.

The use of frameworks is a valuable approach, although it involves a trade-off between greater speed of development and reduced flexibility to design the application to behave exactly as required. Attempts to introduce this approach often run aground as developers and customers insist on requirements that cannot be comfortably accommodated within the constraints of the framework. It is also difficult to achieve a stable framework that does not require change. One danger is that when the framework changes, the application-specific code that builds on the framework may need to be changed. This is a problem that has often been experienced with standard C++ class libraries, sold by software vendors for use when building C++ applications, where early versions have required updates that then impact applications built using them.[1]

1.2.1.2 *Maintainability*

The structures used to assist rapid development have not always helped with maintainability. Code often ends up fragmented between event handlers, triggers, and other types of module. The development tool itself often requires the opening of multiple windows in order to navigate through the program, making

---

1. I am not of course suggesting that these C++ class libraries are 4GLs. With a 4GL, the underlying code framework is usually hidden. The principle of exploiting a standard code framework in multiple applications is similar.

it difficult to obtain an overall picture. Understanding the way the elements fit together in order to debug an application can be tricky.

1.2.1.3 Lack of plug and play

CASE and 4GL tools have a tendency to lock you into their programing approach. It is often assumed that the whole application will be produced using the tool. It is not easy to combine parts of the application produced using a tool with parts produced using a 3GL or with technology other than the CASE vendor's.[2]

Locking the CASE user into a proprietary toolkit makes handling change difficult. The CASE user has no choice but to use the toolkit, while the CASE vendor has single-handedly to keep up with the software industry's fast-changing technology and practices. It is highly unlikely that any CASE vendor can achieve this. But failure is liable to leave the CASE user with applications built using a toolkit that no longer supports current programing technologies, developed by a vendor which has probably gone out of business.

1.2.1.4 Top-down approach

With CASE tools in particular, there is often a tendency to approach the problem top-down, starting with a high-level model of the application and gradually increasing the level of detail until a sufficient level is reached to create a functioning application.

The natural result of this is the development of a new 4GL and an attempt to be all-encompassing – producing lock-in as described above. It also means that most CASE tools stumble at the hurdle of keeping documentation in line with code. The two are liable to diverge.

A more productive approach might be to work on providing computer assistance to a developer who is using a standard programing language. You could work backwards from this to understand how to model the earlier specification phases so that the relevant result is reached. This approach is much easier with an OO language and development method because the gap between the OO programing paradigm and the accepted OO modeling techniques that can be used at earlier stages in the development process is relatively small.

Starting at the programing level might also make it easier to discover how to support a plug-and-play approach in which components built using one CASE tool can play with components built using another one.

1.2.2 Reuse

Reuse has received much attention as a way of improving the efficiency of software development. CBD can be seen as emerging from the same stable.

---

2. Some tools offer reverse engineering and round-trip capabilities allowing models to be created from code. This only really works with the simpler forms of code generation, for instance where code generation is used to generate header files.

Reuse is in some ways a puzzling concept. While occasionally computer programs are written to be run only once, generally programs are intended for reuse as a matter of course. And within a program we reuse code as a matter of course. We use loops so that the same code will execute more than once and we modularize code into subroutines that we invoke from more than one point in the program.

While these facts may seem obvious, they help highlight the truth that, when we talk about reuse, what we mean is that we want to achieve a greater level of reuse than we are already doing. Whatever level of reuse we currently achieve in our development activities, which will vary depending on the organization, when we talk about reuse our idea is to take steps to increase that level.

Reuse can apply to all phases of a project. If you have developed a similar application before, you can often usefully reuse requirement specifications from the earlier project. Designs produced for a previous project can be reused. You can save time by reusing coding standards and other development standards. And usually, when a programer starts writing a new program, he or she will begin by copying an existing program. These are types of reuse that are usually employed in any organization.

One way of increasing the level of reuse is to adopt a standard architecture, as discussed in the previous section on CASE tools and 4GLs. Just as 4GLs often rely on the use of a framework, an organization can decide to use standard framework code and shared subroutine libraries as the basis for applications, reusing these from project to project.

Another way of increasing the level of reuse is to produce more generic code by looking for similar requirements and producing code that covers more than one requirement.

It is often the case that the differences between requirements are the result of historical differences in practice. If it is possible to persuade users to adopt a single common approach, then the reused code can really become the same in all instances, rather than being tailored to each different group within the organization.

Where reused code has to meet a number of requirements that are not quite the same, there are more difficult trade-offs to consider. In these cases, there is a potential benefit from having to maintain only one reusable module, but there is also a danger that maintenance will be more difficult because conditional logic must be introduced to deal with the variations in the logic. The decision to use a common module or specific modules has to balance these advantages and disadvantages.

Where there really is a common model with clearly defined variations, the use of OO techniques can offer real benefits. They allow the common model to be coded in a supertype object while subtypes handle each independent variation, with methods that can override the methods in the supertype where variant logic is required. [3]

3. Inheritance requires careful use. See discussions of subtyping, substitutability, and implementation inheritance in, for instance, *Mainstream Objects* by Ed Yourdon *et al.*, Prentice-Hall, 1995.

Sometimes, something may look reusable because it is referred to by the same term, although in fact the term refers to a whole set of items that have very little reusable overlap. For instance, there is a large number of possible accrual algorithms for calculating how interest is earned. While these serve the same function, basically each algorithm is independent and does not offer much potential for reuse. Limits processing, where a notification should be triggered if a limit is exceeded, is referred to under a single name, but a limit can be applied to virtually everything, from the temperature in a cooling tower to the amount lent worldwide to a given individual.

Interestingly, these are examples of positional reuse. The logic that should be inserted is different; the similarity is in how the logic is invoked. All the different types of accruals processing are usually invoked from the same place in the application. Limits processing applies in multiple different locations in an application, but can always be applied in a similar way. OO techniques can help here too. Given an abstract enough definition of the object on which a limit is required, a single pattern (or a few standard patterns) could be used for providing limits processing. (There are trade-offs here as well – too generic an approach can increase maintenance overheads and performance costs.)

Developers asked to improve reuse sometimes become over-enthusiastic and invest too much effort in designing generic code that covers all alternatives and anticipates future requirements. Given the rate of change of requirements, there is a serious risk that requirements will change in unforeseen ways, so that code developed to anticipate these requirements is simply wasted effort.

There are other downsides to reuse. It generally costs more development effort to develop generic, reusable code. The code may also perform less well than code developed to meet a specific requirement. Maintenance can be more difficult because the code has to cater for variations.

There may also be organizational reasons for not reusing code. If one group is responsible for an application, it may not make sense to reuse code from another part of the organization if this then means longwinded negotiations over maintenance changes.

Another barrier to reuse is the "not-invented-here" syndrome from which developers frequently suffer. Developers look at someone else's work and conclude that they could have done the work much better. In a completed item of work, the defects are usually glaringly obvious, while the limitations of a design that has not yet been produced are not manifest. Consequently, the developer decides to redevelop the item in question rather than reusing the existing code. Regardless of whether a better result is actually achieved or not, the effort involved in the redevelopment work frequently cannot be justified.

1.2.3 Flexibility

Techniques for making code flexible have been particularly important for the developers of application packages. Such product developers aim to sell their software to as many different customers as possible, but must cater for some variations in requirements between those customers. For home users, flexibility is usually provided within limits by offering alternative ways of doing the same thing. Commercial users have greater bargaining power and may be choosing between a package application and one built to meet their specific needs. Consequently, product developers are more likely to be forced into providing mechanisms that allow the customer to tailor the product to meet their specific requirements.

The mechanisms used include:

- Customization points or "user exits." These are points in the code at which call-outs can be made to code that the customer provides, or that the product developer writes for the specific customer.
- Configuration files. These allow the setting of configuration parameters. Some of these may be set once only, when the application is first installed. Others may be changeable after installation.
- Conditional compilation and macros. These allow the application to be built differently depending on requirements.

1.2.4 Corporate-wide information models

In the 1980s and early 1990s, there was a trend toward the development of corporate-wide data models. The objective was that the organization as a whole would move toward a single data model, making integration between applications easier. An integrated information model would help deal with a situation where information about a given customer might be spread through a number of applications and recorded in different ways in each.

While these endeavors did achieve some benefits, producing a common information model proved to be very costly in terms of effort. Different applications often require slightly different angles on the same information and use different terminology to refer to what could be regarded as the same thing. For instance, in the world of financial instruments, such as loans or bonds, there are many dates relating to settlement, funds transfer, the date on which interest starts accruing, and so on, that are named differently for different instruments, even where the purpose of the date is the same. This makes reconciling the application-specific view with the corporate-wide view a less trivial task than it might at first seem to be.

The politics of such an endeavor are also tricky. It is difficult to persuade people from different parts of the organization to agree on compromise solutions that do not meet their needs exactly but allow everyone to use the same information model. The downside is obvious to the parties involved, while the benefits can seem intangible and far from guaranteed.

Also, in simple historical terms, the trend toward centralization within organizations during the 1980s and 1990s was replaced by a trend toward empowering the different parts of the organization. Decentralization enables parts of an organization to concentrate on their business focus without the overhead of agreeing common practices. It becomes essential when the organization gets too introverted and too concerned about common practices, and unable to respond quickly enough to outside stimuli.

A pendulum movement between centralization and decentralization within organizations is probably a fact of corporate life.

1.3   The promise of component-based development

Most attempts to improve software development have focussed on improving the speed of development of new code. However, most of our effort is spent on maintaining software rather than on its initial development. Whenever we change software, we do need to write new code. But, as already discussed, the complexity of source code, and our failure to limit the amount of code affected by any change, make it very difficult to achieve substantial economies in the effort involved in making a change.

However, if we change our focus and think about reusing executable code, rather than reusing and amending source code, there is visible potential to reduce effort. Suppose we could put together applications from pre-built components and make each of those components independent, so that a change to one component would not impact another component? Effort could be saved at once in cases in which the new application could be built from pre-existing components. In addition, effort could be saved down the line, during maintenance, as the ramifications of a change would now be limited so that they affect only the component in question. (Note: this is not to say that changes could not spread to other components, but now they would do this only where there was a genuine business change in each component, not, as previously, just because we could not be sure how much of the code the programer's technical solution happened to affect.)

The benefits of modularization have, of course, been long understood. However, the fact that with components we are reusing executable code means that modularization is much more rigorously enforced than it is when it is attempted at the source code level.

When reusing source code, because the source code is there to be inspected, there is a tendency to build in unnecessary dependencies between modules. This causes problems when one module is changed, maybe unexpectedly impacting another. Using components imposes greater discipline. If the component that is used is not available for change, and its code is not open for inspection, there will be less tendency to build in unnecessary dependencies. Instead, the component will be used in the way that is dictated by its published interface.

Improving maintainability by reducing the amount of code potentially impacted by a change is, in my view, a significant potential benefit of CBD. A second point in favor of CBD is that it helps to address the problem of evolution of software as requirements change and new front ends are required, or the software has to be restructured to meet new needs.

Components carve up the application into smaller chunks, with each component's scope and impact limited to itself. This makes it easier to restructure an application. For instance, the user interface could be replaced (or a new alternative user interface added) while retaining the business logic.

Finally, CBD helps address the application integration problem that has been untouched by most previous approaches. We need an approach that allows us to move forward in an incremental fashion. It is not viable to simply replace a complete software portfolio in one single step. Instead, existing software must be capable of coexisting with new.

The fact that components carve up the application into smaller chunks that are isolated from one another makes it possible to upgrade applications gradually, replacing one component at a time. This contrasts with the current situation where it is often necessary to replace an application as a whole, because the functionality within the application is closely intertwined and cannot be separated into relatively independent parts.

A component-based approach also offers potential for a gradual migration to well-architected applications – essential since organizations cannot afford to replace existing systems in one big bang. New components can interoperate with components that put a façade on existing applications. Over time, the existing applications can then be improved and replaced by components, but there is no requirement to move the whole application forward at once.

1.4   The feasibility of component-based development

There are two not unreasonable responses to those who promote CBD:

1 Isn't this what we've always done? We've always built our applications from parts, haven't we? What's new?

2 While the benefits of CBD may be obvious, who says that we can improve our success in developing components that really are independent of one another and can be mixed and matched? Software isn't like that. It's inevitably monolithic, and where it isn't, we're already componentizing it as far as is possible.

To some extent, CBD can be seen as a culmination of various development practices, including model-based development, OO programing, and reuse, that have developed over the past two decades.

In my view, one of the main benefits of the approach is that it brings into much sharper focus a number of the issues we have faced. Some of these issues are summarized as follows.

● We now explicitly recognize that the era of greenfield development is over. We must now put software together by combining existing and new applications, or parts of applications. Integration of software has become a primary consideration. Recognizing this consciously helps us to move forward because it enables us to focus on the issues and consider how best to resolve them, instead of finding that we are caught by surprise by software integration issues when our attention was elsewhere.

- When you think about how to integrate software effectively, you realize that the units to be combined should be smaller than those traditionally included in a subsystem – and larger than the classes that are developed using an OO approach. Because of this, very few, if any, of us can justifiably claim to have been involved in CBD in the past. We have only just reached the point of appreciating *what* a component should look like. (Component size will be discussed in more detail in the next chapter.)

- If we are to build components of this size that are to act as separable, self-contained units, we need guidance as to how to define components. How do we scope them, what types should we use, how do we fit them together into an architecture, how can we manage the interface between components in such a way as to keep components independent of one another? These are the issues which CBD has to address, and there is a growing body of understanding as to how to address them.

- Once we grasp what is involved in building components that can be combined effectively, it becomes apparent that a planning process is required. For pragmatic reasons, the planning process must be able to reconcile the need for a "grand plan" with the realities of step-by-step development – "big bangs" are out of the question.

Seeing that improving the level of componentization of our software will bring benefits enables us to ask the question: *How can we achieve more componentization of our software?* Simply formulating the question takes us a good step closer to working out the answer.

As for the argument that we already componentize as much as we can, that is doubtful. Even if a component nirvana will never be achievable, it seems clear that we will be able to find ways of improving the extent to which we componentize applications once we agree that this is a worthwhile objective.

2 What are components?

The term "component" in the phrase "component-based development" has a specialized meaning that is more restricted and specific than its meaning in standard English. As is the case with many emerging terms in the field of software development, the exact meaning attributed to it varies depending on who is using the term.

Until there is consensus, we have no choice but to adopt the position of Humpty Dumpty in Lewis Carroll's *Through the Looking-Glass*:

> *"When I use a word," Humpty Dumpty said in a rather scornful tone, "it means just what I choose it to mean – neither more nor less."*

Nevertheless, there is a widespread informal consensus on which I base the definition I use in this chapter. Of course, the proof of the pudding is in the eating. The definition can be shown to be a good one to the extent that the type of components I describe here meet the objective of helping us with the problems described in the previous chapter.

2.1 Definition of a component

2.1.1 Components are pre-built

In standard English, a component is a part, or element, which is combined with other components to create a whole. Usually a component is a distinct and separable item, such that its identity is not wholly lost in the assembly and, if the assembly is disassembled, it can be recovered relatively intact.

I think the idea that is present in standard English – that components are not wholly submerged in the entity in which they are included – is retained in our software-related use of the term. Software components retain separate identities within the runtime software of which they form a part. They are capable of doing this because they are pre-built.

Note that this means that we are focussing specifically on code-level components, and that we will focus on pre-built components, rather than source code units that might be assembled into a program and then compiled.

There is a *de facto* historical reason for this, which is that components built using, for instance, Microsoft's COM (Component Object Model) are like this. There are, however, other reasons why components need to be like this if they are to help us address the problems described in the previous chapter.

One straightforward reason is that using a pre-built component is cheaper than reusing code earlier in the development process, since it cuts out the earlier parts of the development process.

There is another purely pragmatic reason why a component is pre-built. Application integration, and the reuse of existing applications in ways that were not originally anticipated, form a major part of the problem to be solved. These applications are already built at the time at which we decide we have a further integration need. Even if our applications are initially built from components, these applications, and the components they contain, will already be in a built form when the next need to use the application differently emerges. Just as organizations now want applications integrated "non-intrusively," i.e. without code change, so they will in the future for applications we build now, and components must cater for this by being built with non-intrusive reuse in mind.

Another reason relates to maintainability. As discussed in the previous chapter, one of the major reasons why software is costly to maintain is the difficulty of determining how much software will be impacted by a change. Whatever size of application unit we are responsible for building, there is a tendency for that unit to become a monolithic entity. OO software helps you localize change by packaging related functionality together in one place. So OO software can help significantly in handling the software maintenance problem. Unfortunately, while it can do so, the fact is that the developer is still able to see all the code that is used and consequently may build in dependencies on it. As a result, it is still not safe to make a change without inspecting all code that could possibly be affected, and thus the effort involved in making a change remains great.

A component that is pre-built, on the other hand, places a much stronger boundary between components than there is between the classes of an OO application, particularly if the component's source code is not available. As a result, it becomes possible to assume that a change will impact only the component itself, unless there are obvious reasons related to the business logic that make its impact wider. The amount of code inspection required is thus greatly reduced. This point is very significant, and a successful approach to components involves making sure that development practices do not allow this benefit to be compromised.

Finally, by focussing on components as pre-built entities, we give ourselves better opportunities to adopt a gradual approach to evolution. We can start thinking about how we can change one component without necessarily changing another at the same time. We can also change the implementation of a component, even replace the component completely, without affecting its use by other components, provided that the new component offers the same functionality as previously.

2.1.2 Components are black-box, accessible only via their interfaces

A component must also, of course, be capable of interoperating with other components. How it does this is also important.

It is an important characteristic of a component that it is "black-box." Its internals are not visible to us. To use the jargon, it is encapsulated. We are interested only in the functions or "services" that it offers through a defined interface. It is only through this defined interface that the component can be connected with other components.

Thus, in order to use a component, it is necessary to be able to obtain knowledge of its interfaces, either through an accompanying specification or by querying the component for information about the interfaces it offers. This means that the definition of the interface is key to the definition of a component (see "Component specification" on page 34).

2.1.3 Components are separable

The first principle of defining components is *separability*. In order to achieve the benefits we hope for from components, it must be possible to separate a component from its context and use it in another context.[1]

Well-accepted software engineering principles help to achieve this separability:

- the principle of separation of concerns;
- definition of components to have high cohesion and low coupling;
- encapsulation of the component so that knowledge of its internals is not required by other components.

Achieving separability means that we must think carefully about ways in which one component may be dependent on another. For instance, one component might contain a *Product* object while another contains the *Order* object. There is obviously a relationship between *Orders* and *Products* that is significant in business terms. How can we build a system that reflects the relationship – and thus a natural dependency between the components – while maintaining the independence of the components? This is an interesting question that I will come back to later in the book.

---

1. Some authors refer to this as context independence.

2.1.4   Component assembly and deployment

The definition of a component as a pre-built entity means that components are not assembled before compilation but afterwards.

The assembly of components can involve some level of configuration or customization. This means that the same component could be deployed more than once, with different instances of the component behaving differently depending on how they were configured.

In most business contexts, the application is assembled before deployment, although there are also (increasingly) scenarios in which components are identified and linked to only at runtime. For instance, the ability to link to new components at runtime is an important capability of Sun's Jini™. This makes it possible to link to new devices, such as printers and fax machines, as soon as they appear on the network, even though the printer or fax machine might be of a type not previously manufactured.

2.1.5   Component context

Using components implies a need for standardization of development approach on a number of levels: business logic, software infrastructure, and interfacing standards. This is discussed further under "Component environment" on page 23.

2.1.6   Supporting technology

Because components require a supporting environment, component technologies generally provide a runtime environment within which the assembled application can operate as well as tools that assist with the assembly and deployment of components. The supporting runtime environment for components is generally referred to as a "container."

2.1.7   Components: a definition

Consider this definition of components, that gathers the characteristics of a component discussed so far.

> *A software component is a separable piece of executable software, that makes sense as a unit, and can interoperate with other components, within some supporting environment. The component is accessible only via its interfaces and is capable of use as-is, after any necessary installation and configuration procedures have been carried out. In order for it to be combined with other components, it must be possible to obtain details of its interfaces.*

2.2   Component granularity

Components, like sugar, can be thought of as varying in their granularity. You could build an application from very fine-grained components or from coarse-grained components. Granularity can be measured in terms of the amount of functionality a component provides, typically measured as a number of function points. (This is a better measure than the number of lines of code, which naturally varies depending on the programing language.)

While many currently available components are quite small, the potential of more coarse-grained components is higher. Figure 2.1 shows schematically the forces affecting the value of components of different sizes. The scale shows examples of types of component and their relative granularity. This is of course schematic – one operation may in fact be larger than another class.

Figure 2.1 shows that when we come to define components, we should concentrate on identifying coarse-grained components. Reusing a larger component saves more effort, and so larger components have a greater value to the business. Smaller components are more likely to be frequently used, but their use saves less effort. This means that small components are less cost-effective.

The largest type of component would be a pre-built application package.[2] However, while a pre-built application may offer the best economy, it is often a challenge to find one that sufficiently matches requirements to be justified in business terms. (This varies depending on how standardized the business area is. For instance, accounting packages may require little or no change to fit the business.)

In addition, very large components, unless they are themselves componentized, will be inflexible in the face of change, with changes taking longer to achieve. Their inflexibility means that the benefits we are aiming for with CBD are lost, at least within the area of the business they cover. This means that larger

Figure 2.1
Forces affecting the value of a component

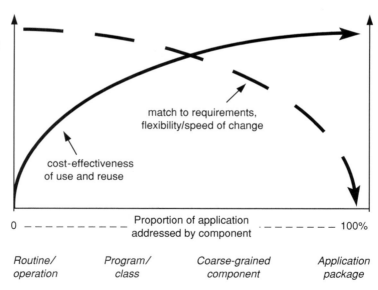

match to requirements, flexibility/speed of change

cost-effectiveness of use and reuse

0 _ _ _ _ _ _ _ _ _   Proportion of application _ _ _ _ _ _ _ 100%
addressed by component

| Routine/ operation | Program/ class | Coarse-grained component | Application package |

2. Generally, an application package will not be a component, as we define it; however, it could in theory be one if it was designed to act as a component in a larger application portfolio.

components should themselves be built in terms of smaller components. And when considering the purchase of a pre-built application, its level of componentization should be carefully considered.

Valuable components may, of course, come in a wide range of sizes, since the best trade-off between size and flexibility will vary according to the component. Nevertheless, the key conclusion to draw from this consideration of component granularity is that the most valuable components will be larger, rather than smaller.

2.3   Component environment

2.3.1   Interoperability

Obviously components are not much use if they can't interoperate. So how can we ensure they do?

The basic requirement is that they must have a common understanding of the interface that they will use, and a common way of describing it. It follows that a standard way of defining the interface between components is needed.

You could, of course, simply build the interface between two components in one way and the interface between another pair of components in a completely different way. This is attractive because it means we can develop in an *ad hoc* fashion, which reduces the amount of thought required – at least initially. The result, however, is components that are not context-independent. If we replace the called component with another component, even with one written in the same language and providing exactly the same functionality, the odds are that its interface will be managed differently. As a result, the code of the calling component will have to be changed. We have now failed to achieve our objective of keeping components separate from one another, such that change to one does not unnecessarily impact another.

This problem becomes more obvious when we consider replacing a component written using one technology with one written in another. Suppose we replace a CICS mainframe component with a Java component that implements exactly the same set of operations. We will have to change the code of each component that calls the new component – even though the actual set of operations provided by the component has not changed.

This problem can be resolved by introducing an agreement on how interfaces will be defined. CORBA, for example, addresses this issue through the use of IDL (Interface Definition Language), which allows interfaces to be specified in a common way regardless of the language in which each component is written.

2.3.2   Interoperability between technologies

While agreement on the interface definition is an important step toward achieving components that are context-independent, we still have to handle the fact that one component might be written using one technology and another using another technology. We need a way of mediating between the calling and called interfaces such that the technology used for one interface can change without impacting the other. This can be achieved by introducing an interface layer that translates between the two technologies.

We could produce interface layers that translate between each possible pair of technologies. However, there could be a large number of possible combinations. A better solution is to use a single technology for the mediating layer. Now we only need to translate into this mediating technology (from the calling technology) and out of this technology (into the called technology). This significantly reduces the number of interface translations that are necessary between different technologies. Where n is the number of different technologies used for different components, the use of a mediating layer reduces the number of interface translations required from $n * (n - 1)$, to $2(n - 1)$.[3] Figure 2.2 shows the effect of introducing a mediating layer.

Note that even with a mediating layer, you could still design your interfaces so that the fact that you are calling a CICS component, say, shows through in the caller. This is poor practice since it compromises the context independence of the components. It shows a failure to create a component that is truly "black box." It should also be avoidable, and where it is not, it suggests that a thicker mediating layer is needed.

2.3.3 Component models

A common component model generally provides a mediating layer of the sort described in the previous section, as well as an agreement as to how interfaces will be defined. If all components are built using COM, or CORBA, or EJB, then

Figure 2.2

Interfaces with and without a mediating layer

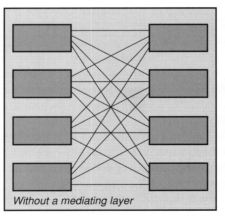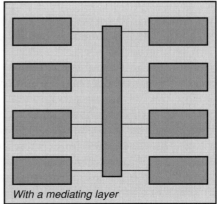

Without a mediating layer   *With a mediating layer*

3. This calculation takes into account the fact that two components implemented using the same technology require no interface translation – thus only $n - 1$ translations are required. It is also assumed that some components use the same technology as the mediating layer.

the interfaces of each component will be defined in a standard way that can be understood by other components that use the same component model.

It is, of course, feasible to use your own component model, rather than a standard one. Is this an option worth considering?

As component models are still immature, it is still possible to argue in favor of building your own component model. This is at least under your own control and can be built to meet your organization's specific needs. The major disadvantage is that it limits the potential for interoperability with components bought from third parties, or with another organization's components for business-to-business applications. Also, it is much more likely that the dominant component model of the future will derive from one of the available component models of today rather than from an in-house component model.

Using a component model works as long as all the components you want to connect use the same component model, or a component model that is capable of interfacing with other component models. Otherwise, you get the same interoperability issue between the component models. You then need a component model to mediate between the component models. Think about it: the same problem could potentially recur *ad infinitum*!

2.3.4   Wrapping existing applications

We need our existing software to work in our component environment, even though it has probably not been written to do so and therefore does not have interfaces defined that conform to the standard defined by the component model we choose to use. To handle this, we will need to put façades on our existing software to enable it to operate within the component environment.

A wrapper can provide a standard component interface on one side, while on the other side it interfaces with the existing application code in a way that is specific to the existing application code. The wrapper, with the existing application code it uses, forms a virtual component that I shall call a "legacy" component. Since other components access the legacy component via a standard component interface, it looks like any other component to them. Now, when we need to change the interface to the existing software for technical reasons, we simply need to change the wrapper, of which there is only one, instead of having to change all the components that use the component. We can rewrite the CICS component in Java without impacting any of the component's clients – only the wrapper is affected. See Figure 2.3 for a schematic representation of this.

This addresses interface issues, but the capabilities of the legacy component may be restricted – for instance, it might not be possible for it to participate in a transaction that has been started by its caller. Component models need to cater for the possibility that some components will have restricted capabilities.

2.3.5   Platform independence

Platform independence, as such, is not a necessary characteristic of a component. All that is needed is that components located on different platforms

Figure 2.3

Putting a component
façade on an existing
application

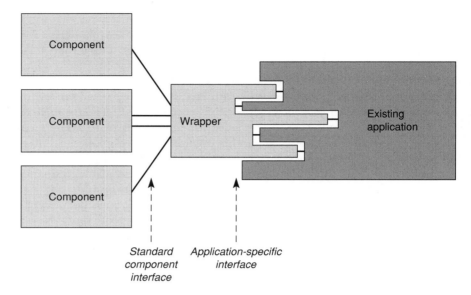

Standard
component
interface

Application-specific
interface

should be able to interoperate. It is perfectly valid for a component to be able to run on only one platform.

Obviously, lack of platform independence restricts the ways in which a component can be reused. Where an organization's requirements are such that the same component is required on more than one platform, there will be a strong motivation to use a language, such as Java, that makes the component, or the component source, portable rather than rewriting the component for each platform.

2.3.6   Provision of services

Component models assist by providing a standardized way of defining component interfaces. In addition, they (increasingly) provide extra runtime support for components.

Providing an infrastructure to handle aspects such as transaction management and security makes it easier to manage the cross-component implications of these aspects of an application. Transactions, for instance, must be able to include updates from multiple components. It is also desirable for them to be able to update databases from different vendors on different platforms. To achieve this, coordination is needed and this coordination is best located outside the individual components – in the infrastructure so that participation in transactions can change without impacting the component. Security, similarly, raises many integration issues. The requisite is either a common security infrastructure – possible within a single component environment – or the ability to map between security systems. The latter is a necessity when integrating existing applications.

In addition, an infrastructure that offers enhanced runtime support makes it easier for component writers to concentrate on business logic rather than on plumbing.

Using a component model that offers more support does, however, impose further standardization on the writers of the components themselves. Components must then be written so that they can take advantage of the facilities offered by the component model.

2.4   Components and their place in a whole

Components are expected to fit into a whole. That whole has to be defined and each component given a scope that ensures its independence within the whole, as previously explained in Section 2.1.3 on page 20.

Defining components as separable entities within a preconceived whole makes it possible to achieve the maintainability benefits offered by components. It also makes it possible to envisage reuse of components in specific scenarios, such as requirements for new user interfaces, or changes in the structure of an organization.

However, one of the touted benefits of components is being able to purchase them from third parties. And one increasingly important requirement is to be able to integrate applications not just within a single organization but with other organizations within the supply chain, to enable "just-in-time" ordering, for example, maybe using what have become known as "Web services."

Application integration techniques can help us fit together parts that were not meant to work together, helping us to translate between different vocabularies. However, the components we create using these techniques do still need to fit together into a coherent picture.

While it helps to have a standardized view within the organization, it will become increasingly important for each industry to improve its level of standardization, both of:

● business concepts themselves and their relationships and interactions; and
● the most effective componentization of a given business domain, so that changes to requirements do not necessitate a change in component boundaries.

This will make it increasingly possible to use components built outside the organization, and to integrate with other businesses' applications and services.

Efforts to standardize business concepts are being made by a number of organizations and consortia. For example, OASIS[4] is an organization that collects business-related standards initiatives across industry as a whole including, to take one example, standards developed by ACORD, a not-for-profit standards association for the insurance industry. As another example, RosettaNet is a non-profit consortium that aims to define standard interfaces for electronic business.

4. The Organization for the Advancement of Structured Information Standards, at www.oasis-open.org

2.5   Deploying components

Before components are deployed they must be developed and assembled, where the developer of individual components may not be the person (or team) that assembles the components. Deployment issues must be addressed during the development and assembly phases, as well as at the time of deployment of the application itself.

2.5.1   Customization and configuration

Because components may be deployed by someone other than their developer, it is important to provide formalized configuration mechanisms. Because they may be used in multiple contexts, it is also important that they can be customized to fit into the specific context in which they are used.

Customization can be achieved by:

- providing configuration data that can be used to parameterize the way a component operates;

- building a configuration or customization service into the component. Such configuration services may be available only during assembly or deployment, and may be disabled or removed for live running of the component.

The process of configuring a component can be made much more user-friendly by providing a component assembly environment. The assembly environment can provide a user interface for setting configuration data and can invoke any configuration service that is provided, supporting the application assembler or deployer in carrying out the configuration process.

This type of configuration service is discussed, for instance, in the JavaBeans™ specification, although it is not mentioned in the Enterprise JavaBeans specification. The JavaBeans specification envisages the use of:

- property sheets, that provide access to properties that can be used to customize the appearance and behavior of the bean, both during the build process, using a design environment, and at runtime, through programatic access;

- a customizer class that the bean developer optionally makes available to assist in the customization of the bean.

Once the component has been configured, the configured options must be stored so that they can be reloaded when the component is used.

2.5.2   Assembly: Gluing components together

If you put together two components that were designed to work together, presumably they will simply fit. One component will invoke a service offered by another component and the arguments required will match those supplied. If you put together two components that were not originally designed to work together, they still need to have a reasonable fit in order for the assembly to work.

It should be possible to determine the degree of fit from the component specification produced when the component is developed initially, which should define the interface the component provides and some other aspects relevant to the deployment of the component – principally constraints on how it can be deployed, such as what operating system the component will run on and what component services it requires.

Assuming a component does provide a required service with a reasonable degree of fit and its deployment constraints can be catered for, some mapping between the two interfaces may still be required. "Glue" is the code that sits between two interfaces and makes them fit.

What might not fit?

- The parameters might be passed in a different order to that expected by the called service.

- The called service might require a parameter that the caller does not supply.

- The caller might supply parameters that the called service does not require.

- The format in which parameters are required might be different from that in which parameters are passed, or a different value might be used – for instance, the caller might identify a person using his or her social security number while the called service identifies a person using some other value.

The same mapping issues apply to the values returned to the caller by the service.

The use of XML[5] has been heavily promoted as a way of handling some of these differences. XML is used to mark up data with labels that indicate the data's meaning. For instance, the label "phonenum" might be used for a phone number. While HTML describes data in terms of how it is to be displayed and interacted with, XML simply tags data, leaving its processing (for display or any other purpose) to the recipient of the data.

XML offers the following main benefits.

1 It disposes of the problem presented by an interface that passes parameters by position. Since each parameter is identified by a tag, the order in which parameters are passed does not have to match the order in which the called service specifies them. The mapping can be managed without a dependency on the order.

2 As tags are used to label each field, these tags can be used to associate semantics with each field. A field can be identified as a customer number, for instance. Mappings from one value to another are possible and could be specified in a dictionary. They could involve looking up data in a database in order to transform the value supplied by the caller into a value of the

---

5. XML (Extensible Markup Language) is a generalized markup language based on SGML (Standard Generalized Markup Language), and influenced by HTML, that is targeted primarily at the Web. XML is extensible in that the set of markup symbols to be used is not limited. See the World Wide Web Consortium (W3C) for more information on XML.

type required by the called service (e.g. mapping between different customer identifier formats used in different parts of an organization).

3 Assuming the use of XML, vocabularies can be standardized, both within an organization and between businesses. This has led to the use of XML for the standardization of business vocabularies. Where business vocabularies expressed in XML do not match, XML offers a means of translating between dialects, using XSL transformations. [6]

Of course, XML is not the only possible solution to these mapping issues, but it is one that is becoming widely adopted, for example for use in Web service interfaces, and this makes it an even more compelling candidate for use.

In more complicated cases, there are other aspects that may not map between calling component and called service, particularly when integration with existing legacy applications is involved. There could be a mismatch between the granularity of services, such that:

● where the calling component expects one call to a single service to suffice, it might be necessary to call more than one service;

● it might not be possible to call a service until more information has been supplied.

There could be a mismatch in expectation as to how a request should be handled. For instance, the caller might want a synchronous response to its request, while the called service operates at intervals on files of batched-up requests.

These more complicated cases usually call for a wrapper, as explained in Section 2.3.4 on page 25. The wrapper together with the wrapped application are best viewed as a new "logical" component. This makes it possible to replace the combination later with a component that fits better.

A world of application integration tools is emerging that helps with the process of building wrappers, adapters, and connectors to existing applications.

As far as possible, it is best to use a consistent overall component reference model, which defines what components there should be and the services they should offer, and work toward creating components that fit this model, rather than simply fitting items together in an *ad hoc* fashion. This makes it easier to reconnect components as the need arises and creates a simpler overall picture than the one that results from an *ad hoc* approach, where components are liable to cut up functionality in ways that clash.

2.5.3   Handling change

There are various possible strategies for handling change to components, whether these changes are due to bug fixes or enhancements. Bug fixes should generally not involve changes to interfaces or to the specification, whereas enhancements may well involve such changes.

---

6. XSL Transformations (XSLT) provide a standard way to describe how to transform the structure of an XML document into an XML document with a different structure. See the World Wide Web Consortium (W3C) for more information on XSLT.

Changes to components can raise particular issues where a component is used in more than one context. In such cases, it may well be that the change made in one context is not acceptable in another – not because it wouldn't work but because the upgrade would involve retesting and an element of risk. In these cases, there is a requirement for a "non-intrusive" approach to change. This makes it essential to be able to deploy different versions of the same component.

Similar issues arise where more than one component makes use of the services of a component that has been modified. If a change that is relevant for one client involves a change to the component's interface, it is desirable that other clients should be unaffected by the change.

One approach to this (which is the one recommended in Microsoft's COM) is to freeze interfaces that have been published for use. The component must continue to offer the interface. When a new requirement emerges that cannot be met using that interface, the component simply offers a new interface in addition to the previous one.

In my opinion, this approach of not withdrawing an interface should be adopted generally. The changes, however, can be rung on the mechanism used to avoid withdrawing the old interface. For instance, where XML is used together with glue that maps the caller's interface to the called interface, called interfaces can be *extended* without impacting the caller. This means that, providing only extensions are required, both the old and new requirements can be met using a single interface.

2.6   Component models

This section provides a thumbnail sketch of the advantages and disadvantages of three major component models:

- MTS and COM, part of Microsoft's .NET
- the CORBA Component Model (CCM) and CORBA
- EJB and Java.

These are not covered in much technical depth but simply in terms of their key differences.

COM, CORBA (Common Object Request Broker Architecture), and Java all make it possible to develop and run distributed components. MTS (Microsoft Transaction Service), CCM, and EJB enhance the capabilities provided by COM, CORBA, and Java by providing improved support for deploying components and improved runtime environments. It is important to note that these extended models specifically target the needs of *server-side* components.

The extended component models provide additional runtime support in the following areas.

- Transaction management. The ability to handle distributed transactions. Components can manage transactions themselves, or can leave transaction management to be handled implicitly by the container.

- Security management. Security inevitably raises many integration issues. Either a common security infrastructure or an ability to map between security systems is needed.

- Management of persistent data. In EJB and CCM (but not COM) the container can be made responsible for ensuring that persistent data is saved in the database (or other data store).

- Instance management, database connection pooling, threading, state management, etc. These aspects all relate to ways in which the container can ensure efficient use of computer resources so that applications perform well and scale well as more users connect to an application. These are aspects traditionally associated with transaction processing monitors but now also supplied by a good component environment.

One factor that makes it easier for these component models to provide the above services is that the technologies used handle the communications between components (enabling transparent distribution of components). This makes it possible for them to intercept communications and to add in their own services at the interception point.

While COM can run on some non-Microsoft platforms (e.g. Unix), it is a widely accepted model only on Windows. Java can run on any platform that supports the Java virtual machine, while CORBA can run on any platform on which a particular object request broker (ORB) product can run (which, for many ORBs, includes all platforms that support a Java Virtual Machine (JVM).

2.6.1   COM and MTS

COM is Microsoft's architecture for component software. COM defines a binary standard for component interoperability within and across process boundaries through interfaces that are independent of implementation languages. Implementations based on COM include Microsoft ActiveX (previously OLE) for component software services, MTS for transaction services, and OLE DB for data access services.

2.6.2   CORBA

CORBA is a standard for ORBs produced by the OMG (the Object Management Group).[7] ORBs are products that enable objects to transparently make requests and receive responses in a distributed heterogeneous environment.

The CORBA standard makes it possible to write objects (or components) in different languages, such as Java and C++, and for these to interoperate transparently, without any awareness that the component communicated with is written in a different language. Similarly, objects require no knowledge of

---

7. The OMG is a software consortium whose main objective is to establish an architecture and set of specifications to enable distributed integrated applications.

whether another object is on the same host machine or what operating system is used.

A main advantage of CORBA as compared with COM is that COM is focussed mainly on Windows environments, while CORBA works on multiple different operating systems. The CORBA model is platform and language-independent.

One often mentioned disadvantage of CORBA, as compared with COM, is that it is not a binary standard. In the past this has affected the ability to port server-side components written using CORBA from one ORB vendor's implementation to another. However, for ORBs that conform to the newer versions of the CORBA standards (2.3 and later), while CORBA is still not a binary standard, server-side components are now portable due to the introduction of the POA (portable object adapter).

The fact that CORBA is not a binary standard does make it more costly for ORB vendors to support every variant of every possible language compiler on every platform. For this reason, the number of platforms, languages, and compiler variants supported by each ORB vendor is usually limited. COM components can be written in more languages than CORBA components. On the other hand, CORBA components can be deployed on more platforms.

2.6.3 Enterprise JavaBeans and JavaBeans

Enterprise JavaBeans (EJB) is a server-side component model, while JavaBeans is a completely unrelated model that is intended for use *intra*-process rather than for distributed components. JavaBeans is used primarily to build client software and caters for GUI widgets (as well as non-GUI code).

EJB is a standard developed by Sun Microsystems, with the idea that multiple vendors could offer EJB server environments, just as multiple vendors offer CORBA implementations.

Many EJB servers use CORBA under the wrappers, and EJB and CORBA standards seem to be becoming more and more closely aligned. The EJB 1.1 specification includes a mapping to CORBA and states that "a later release of the J2EE platform is likely to require that the J2EE platform vendor implement the EJB to CORBA mapping."

The EJB to CORBA mapping includes the use of IIOP (the underlying CORBA message-passing protocol) for remote method calls and for the propagation of transaction and security context, as well as the use of the interoperable naming service. EJB also relies on CORBA for its transaction support. It assumes the use of the JTS (Java Transaction Service), which is a Java binding of the CORBA Object Transaction Service (OTS) specification.

The CORBA component model includes EJB amongst the types of component supported, and specifies further support over and above that provided by EJB. The two standards may play leapfrog.

The main disadvantage of EJB is that it requires all components to be written in Java. Given Java's current dominance, this may not seem like a problem. It does, however, present issues in relation to legacy integration. Java programs must run in a JVM. This can make it difficult to use Java for tight integration with non-Java code. When the integrating code should run in the same process space as the integrated code, C or C++ can be less problematic to use.

2.7   Component specification

This section outlines some of the possible characteristics that could be defined as part of a component specification. Not all the aspects outlined here are available with every component model.

A component's interface definition defines how the component is perceived by a client and how the client can interact with it. A useful component interface definition will specify:

- the interfaces it offers for use by a client, including details of any exceptions that may be raised;
- any interfaces it requires its client to support (so that it can invoke operations in the client);
- the interfaces it requires from other components, so that the component assembler can make sure that suitable components are available.

Interfaces may include both synchronous and asynchronous interfaces. Also (as part of its interface), a component may raise events, or itself subscribe to events that are raised by other components.[8]

It is useful if component developers provide further information about component interfaces in a form that can be used by a component assembler. For instance, a description of each operation is necessary so that a component assembler can determine whether a component can be used to supply a required service. The operation description should include at least an informal expression of pre- and post-conditions.

In addition, other component characteristics must be specified, including:

- statefulness, re-entrancy, ability to serve multiple clients;
- whether the component requires a new transaction, is capable of operating within an existing transaction, etc.;
- whether the component writes data to the database or not;
- customization capabilities;
- security options;
- operating requirements (e.g. operating system, space required, etc.).

---

8. The EJB 2.0 specification provides a new type of bean, messaging beans, which handle asynchronous communications, while the CORBA component model caters for events.

Putting components in perspective 3

CBD is just one weapon in an armory of techniques for improving our effectiveness at software development. Components mean we focus on a good partitioning of software at the *executable* level. This is only one part of the whole picture. In order to be successful with CBD – or indeed with any other approach to software development – we must pay attention to other important aspects, including:

- ensuring that the organization deploys people effectively – the *sine qua non* of software development;
- using good analysis and program planning techniques to ensure that software solutions meet the real business needs;
- the adoption of specification techniques that enable "model-based" development, including the use of patterns and the reuse of existing specifications;
- the maintenance of an effective development environment that enables efficient management of all project phases and overall control of the whole application portfolio, from specification through to deployed applications;
- the development of a powerful software infrastructure (architecture, frameworks, generators, standard code) to shorten development timescales and improve quality;
- effective project management techniques.

All these aspects together are necessary parts of a disciplined approach to software development, and CBD does require a disciplined approach if success is to be achieved. In many ways, CBD emerges from and builds on our experience over the past decades with development methods, OO techniques, reuse, infrastructures, frameworks, and the automation of the development process. All of this experience is relevant to CBD.

This chapter discusses the relationship between CBD and some of these other development techniques, as well as looking at how organizational context affects the relevance of components.

3.1 The relevance of model-based development

There is an interesting tension between two attitudes toward CBD. Some people believe an integrated, centralized approach is essential. If components are like the parts of a jigsaw puzzle, then we can hardly expect them to fit together if we haven't designed the overall puzzle. Without an overall design, the parts simply won't fit.

Those who want to purchase components from a third party, on the other hand, would like to make these purchases on an *ad hoc* basis. For them it would be a huge disadvantage if an overall design was required.

A further group of people look at the problem primarily from an application integration perspective. To these, it is essential that parts that do not fit should be made to do so. A master plan is seen as meaning tight integration between components, with each component designed to fit exactly with the needs of another. But for application integration, techniques and technologies are needed that allow components to be loosely coupled. A requirement for an overall master plan seems to run counter to this and to imply that it is not possible to patch applications together into a new whole.

If you have a focus on application integration (and from a pragmatic point of view such a focus is essential), it is easy to dismiss those who believe that an overall model is required as impractical purists, still pursuing new development projects in a world in which the era of greenfield development is over.

But consider the consequences of *ad hoc* development. The same considerations apply both when incorporating third-party components and when integrating applications, so I will specifically consider the issues associated with application integration.

Suppose that we evolve our applications based on the shape they already have, without giving much consideration to how each existing application fits into the overall picture. To address new business requirements, it will inevitably prove necessary to create new applications by building new application front ends that interface with business logic contained in existing applications. When this happens, the obvious approach will be to define interfaces to the legacy application at the points at which the structure of the legacy application makes interfaces readily possible. The simplest approach will simply structure the new application front end in such a way that it can use these interfaces.

This approach makes the structure of the application front end dependent on the practicalities of interfacing with the legacy application. Because of our *ad hoc* approach, we will probably also build into the application front end whatever knowledge it needs to have of the physical implementation of the legacy application in order for it to function. So the application front end we would build for a different implementation of the same business logic would have to be different.

This approach limits the potential for moving the application portfolio forwards. It has a number of deficiencies.

1 The new application front end builds in knowledge of the existing application's design. It is exposed to any deficiencies that the existing application's design may suffer from. It does not separate concerns, so that the impact of any change is likely to be spread between new and old code in an unpredictable way. Any person carrying out maintenance will need to understand both the new and the legacy application in order to make changes.

2 We have allowed the location of easy interface points to determine the structure of our new application. This is unlikely to result in a good, maintainable architecture.

3 We have built a local solution. We have done nothing to move the application portfolio as a whole toward more reusable components, with a reduction in redundancy, etc. It is unlikely that the misshapen components we have now produced will be reusable in other contexts. The result of our work offers no improved potential for rearchitecting the original legacy application.

A more structured approach to reusing and reengineering legacy code, on the other hand, would help improve the level of componentization of the application portfolio, with all the benefits that this brings.

To achieve this, we should aim to give the new application an architecture that is not based on the structure of existing legacy code but on the requirements of the new application. We should design the application's architecture to fit in with the overall architecture toward which we aim to move the application portfolio as a whole.

By building in terms of the components that we wish to have in the long term, even if we implement these components only partially, we move the architecture of the application portfolio in the planned direction. Our new components "wrap" the interfaces with the legacy application. They have the shape and scope we want for future use. They also present a standard interface to the outside world, so that exposure to the idiosyncrasies of the legacy application is reduced.

Thus there *is* a requirement for an architected approach, even when focussing on application integration. This in turn makes model-based development an important part of any CBD strategy, as it offers a way to model and manage the overall picture. The overall model provides an overall game plan. It is also useful when assembling components, as it makes it possible to see what components are required for a given application and whether a potential component meets requirements.

3.2   Specification and design reuse

The following types of reusable artefact can be useful during the specification and design process, as part of model-based development:

- reference models
- design patterns.

Reference models may be used both to identify and define components and component interfaces. They are particularly useful for business analysis.[1] Matching requirements to the reference model allows the developer to gain a more complete and rigorous understanding of those requirements. Reference models may be provided by vendors or built within an organization.

A design pattern explains a general design that addresses a recurring design problem. It describes both the problem and possible solutions. Solutions are often described in terms of possible standard patterns for the interaction between objects/components. To solve a specific design problem, the pattern is applied to the problem to create a specific, concrete result. Design patterns make it possible to carry out design activities more quickly and effectively by reusing standard building techniques.

These complementary techniques can be used in conjunction with CBD.

3.3   The relevance of object-oriented techniques

CBD requires that you build well-encapsulated generic parts. A component should have a well-defined interface that can be expressed in terms of services that can be requested from the component, and services that the component can request from other components. It is logical that the component, like an object, must contain both the data and the operations that act on that data. Thus a component has the same external characteristics as an object.

More significantly, the OO design principles that assist in ensuring that an object is well-encapsulated, redundancy is avoided, and the effect of changes is localized to the relevant object type are also important for component-based design.

Differences are:

- a component will often be larger in scope than a class. Its scope may include a number of classes or object types;[2]

---

1. Business analysis involves building an application-independent representation of a business domain for which applications may be built. More generically, this activity is referred to as domain analysis, where the domain that is analyzed might be a business domain but might, for instance, be word processing or a compiler.
2. In a component-based system, a component may also contain only one aspect of an object type, just as, in an OO system, behavior belonging to one object type might be split between classes in different subsystems.

- the internal design of the component can either be OO or not, as long as the component looks like an object from the outside;[3]

- it is possible to envisage a component-based paradigm that does not use inheritance (although this is not a necessary restriction);[4]

- CBD puts more emphasis on black-box reuse than OO development. Usually OO developers are free to look inside classes they use, and can negotiate changes with fellow developers. With components, the internal design may not be available (perhaps because the component was purchased) and change cannot be so easily negotiated. This means that CBD requires more formal specification of the semantics as well as the syntax of a component's interface, and better defined techniques for finding and reusing components than OO does.

Given the relevance of OO design principles, a method for defining components naturally builds on the understanding acquired through OO practice of the best ways to separate functionality into independent components. Note that this does not imply that components themselves must be object-oriented or that an OO development technology must be used to develop components. On the contrary, it is essential to the objectives of CBD (because of the need to address application integration) that non-OO components should be usable, while use of OO components remains a matter of choice.

3.4 Software infrastructure and development automation

It should already be clear from the previous two chapters that components and the use of a software infrastructure that supports components go hand in hand. Thus, CBD continues the trend toward formalizing standard application architectures and building applications based on frameworks.

The fact that the developer of a component will often be different from the person who assembles a component-based application, and the need to configure the way the component is used in the assembled application, mean that development automation also plays an important role.

The specification of EJB recognizes the role of development automation in its assumption that container providers will also provide deployment tools.

---

3. Any given component can be built using either an OO or a non-OO development technology. For CBD, it is desirable to be able to utilize both types of component.
4. Various technologies allow the definition of a component that inherits from another component.

3.5   Differing needs of different types of organization

Different types of organization have different needs with respect to components, i.e. software houses, product vendors, end users.

End users want a set of components that fit together. To keep costs down, however, they are likely to wish to buy third-party components or packages. They are also likely to want to outsource development projects as a way of handling bulges in demand, or as a way of avoiding the need to maintain a large software development department. End users stand to gain from an increase in the number of components that are commercially available, but for them the issue of standardization across the industry is particularly important. Buying components from different sources and then finding that they cannot interoperate is not an attractive option.

When an end-user organization outsources a development project, it will be simplest to let the outsourcer develop the application in isolation, without considering how the new application fits into the overall application portfolio. The logistics of outsourcing make it desirable that the software to be developed has as few interfaces with other software as possible. However, this makes it difficult to move the application portfolio on to a better architected state overall.

Ideally the outsourcer will be instructed to work within the end-user organization's defined framework and set of constraints. However, the outsourcer will often charge more for this, anticipating problems fitting in with standards that are not well defined and likely to be in a process of change. This can create a tension between the department commissioning the specific application, which wants the application delivered as speedily and simply as possible, and the needs of the organization overall.

Depending on the organization, and the level of independence of the individual business departments, there may be no opportunity to ensure that the outsourcer takes into account the organization's application portfolio as a whole when designing the application.

The software houses that provide outsourced applications have themselves to deal with multiple users. They can benefit if they can reuse, for the next customer, software that has been developed for a previous customer. In order to achieve this, they are likely to have a stronger focus on the need to create customizable components than an end user. The end user only needs components that work within the context of his or her own organization and so is likely to be less concerned about the ability to customize components for use in different contexts. (The end user may still have an interest in customization, particularly in large organizations that, in fact, incorporate a number of separate businesses.)

Product vendors share with software houses the need to make their components independent and parameterizable. They need ways of tailoring each component to meet the needs of different users. An important question for product vendors is the issue of how the product is best sold. Is it best to provide a bundled package, with componentization being used internally solely to provide maintainability and flexibility for the product vendor, or will purchasers see value in buying separate components?

Selling software as components can reduce the strains on the product vendor's own development organization, making the release process less traumatic as smaller items are easier to release. On the other hand, selling smaller items costs more and may reduce profits, or require a different selling model.

3.6 Where component-based development is not relevant

CBD is not relevant in all development contexts. Examples of cases where it is not relevant are:

- where change isn't expected;
- where software is not heavily used;
- start-ups that cannot afford it;
- where you have no available talent;
- where time pressures are such that you cannot do it.

In the following, I consider each of these possibilities in more detail.

Some parts of the application portfolio are likely to be very static. The applications in question may be used quite heavily, but the level of change required is low. In this case, there is little reason to move toward componentizing the software. The same is true of software that is used only occasionally. The requirement for change is likely to be low and the return on the investment of moving to a componentized approach is not likely to make such a change worthwhile.

Start-ups might well benefit from componentization. They are likely to face application integration problems as they fit existing packages together, and may well need the flexibility and adaptability in the face of change that a componentized approach would give. A start-up company with good funding, operating in a high-tech area, that sees its competitive advantage as coming from the applications that support its business, will probably invest in componentized software and a sophisticated approach to software architecture. Other start-ups are not likely to see this as a high priority.

CBD requires reasonably sophisticated development staff, who are able to work within a team environment that requires the use of a standard development approach. Even more importantly, it depends on the existence of key individuals within the organization who have the vision to be able to create a component-based architecture, and the leadership ability and credibility within the organization to be able to orchestrate the implementation of that vision. Without such people, an attempt to introduce CBD is unlikely to be successful.

3.7   Limitations of component-based development

While the potential benefits of componentizing software are obvious, the extent to which these can be achieved is not clear. Developers generally do try to modularize their software, but there has still been only limited success in achieving a modularization that really does mean that the impact of change does not spread. Changing requirements have a tendency to necessitate a completely different software structure to the one that was anticipated.

The objective of being able to slot bought components into a coherent application obviously has its limits. It will work only if there is a consensus as to how a particular business area should be broken down into components. We have yet to achieve the level of standardization required to make this consensus possible.

The breaking up of a software application into a set of components is a problem. If you define a set of components, you define how the problem space should be broken up. This may be just about possible for a single problem area, but it seems less likely that it could be done for multiple problem spaces and multiple contexts. Each one is likely to cut up the problem space slightly differently. It is, after all, a complex world out there.

In addition to these intrinsic problems, it is a fact that CBD is still at an early stage. This means that few standards exist to enable the development of components that could address the business domain in a consistent way, and the component technologies that can be used (e.g. CORBA, EJB, COM) are also at relatively early stages in their development. It is also a fact that the number of components that can be bought is small. All these factors make it more difficult to move toward components than it would be if the standards and technologies were more mature and the market for components better developed.

As I said in Chapter 1, while these issues do exist, the fact that success will have its limits does not mean that we cannot make progress. Despite these factors, I think it is well worthwhile to try to move more toward CBD, because even partial success should bring benefits.

The planning process

Positioning components within the organization

4

No useful development effort occurs in a vacuum. So it is important to think carefully about how the adoption of components fits within the organizational context of a business. It is worth asking how the way the business is organized will impact on how components can be used. Is it possible, or probable, that the business's organization will limit what can be achieved? It is also desirable to consider how to organize the collaboration between the business side of the organization and the IT department so that the increased use of components brings as much benefit as possible.

To simplify the discussion, I will focus primarily on the issues facing an end-user organization. The issues facing a software house or a product development organization are different but sufficiently similar for it to be possible for any interested reader to extrapolate from one type of environment to the others.

4.1 The ownership and scope of a component-based development initiative

Two factors seem to be key in determining the right scope for a CBD initiative.

1 The scope of control of the sponsor of the initiative – whatever the position of the initiative's sponsor, it is pointless to try to manage a development initiative with a scope that extends beyond his or her scope of control. This is the simple reality of working within an organization. If you are an employee wishing to influence company direction, or a consultant advising an organization, this seemingly obvious point should provoke you into considering who you are seeking to influence and what their scope of control is!

2 The development initiative needs to be limited to a size that can be successfully managed, while not being so limited in scope as to bring no benefits.

Who might sponsor the initiative? Possible answers are:

- a business unit

- the IT department

- the organization as a whole (or a subsidiary organization as a whole).

If the sponsor is a business unit, and the business unit operates independently, the natural outcome will be that the business unit will adopt an approach that brings it benefits, but may not deliver benefits to other parts of the business. While this puts bounds on what can be achieved, it is also the easiest model to manage. Within the business unit, a homogeneous model of the business unit's software systems can be created, as well as a software infrastructure.

If the sponsor is the IT department, the scope of the initiative will depend on the nature of the IT department's remit within the organization as a whole. It is often the case that control over IT decisions is devolved to individual business units. Where this is true, the IT department's scope for initiative can be quite limited. On the other hand, there may be high-level backing for a coordinated approach to IT across a number of business units, in which case it may be possible for the IT department to develop a software model that spans business units. This wider scope gives greater potential for the efficient use of a component-based architecture.

A third possibility is that there could be a corporate-level sponsor who is able to back a coordinated approach across business units. Whether this is likely depends on the position of the corporate pendulum on its swing between a decentralized and a centralized approach to management. This pendulum is no doubt affected by trends or fashion, but also by corporate perception of the balance between the economies that a centralized approach can deliver and the slowing of speed of response, bureaucratic overheads, and failure to empower that a centralized approach tends to cause.

With a centralized approach, the possibility of coordinating software systems across a number of business units can be considered. A software model that spans the requirements of the different business units can be created. A good match between the software structure and the organizational structure will provide the key to success.

Where cooperation between business units is desired but a more decentralized approach is favored, it will be relevant to consider setting up an internal market for components, as discussed later in this chapter.

4.2   Coordinating software across organizational units

Where a centralized approach is possible, it is necessary to consider what level of coordination is useful. What are the similarities and dissimilarities between the needs of different business units?

For instance, an organization may have a head office with a significant number of branch offices that essentially operate the same business. Each branch may operate more or less autonomously but have very similar software requirements because its business is the same as that of other branches. In this case, using a common software infrastructure makes sense because of the potential for cost savings.

Where an organization is made up of a number of different businesses, there may nevertheless be synergy between the businesses which is best exploited through a coordinated reuse of software. Common access to sales information could be of benefit, or customers may require a single view of their dealings with the company, or order-fulfillment mechanisms could be shared. There may also be opportunities for cost savings by using the same software.

These points should make it apparent that the key reasons for coordinating software are – or should be – business ones. The best reasons are not based on any ideological view that "components are a good thing" but on real business needs. A component-based view merely makes it easier to meet business needs in a flexible way.

4.2.1   Matching software structure with the organization

When stovepipe applications were originally developed, they matched the structure of the organization well. Each application was typically developed for the organizational unit that needed it. Thus, ownership was not an issue.

Imagine an overall component blueprint that allocates ownership for each component to a specific business unit. The ideal result would be that the structure of the organization and the structure of the software were found to mirror one another.

For instance, there could be a part of the organization, say customer care, that is responsible for interactions with customers and for maintaining information about customers. The software for maintaining customer information should be owned by the part of the organization responsible for customer interactions, in this case the customer care unit. Every other part of the organization, of course, is also likely to need access to information about customers. Usually, this can be achieved by allowing other units to use customer care's application to access this information. The result is that there is only one version of the software that requires maintenance and change. Change management consequently becomes less problematic.

Mapping components to the organization can reveal areas where it is difficult to unequivocally assign ownership. This could well indicate that the organization requires improvement and that the structure of the organization should be changed. With a well-designed organization, software structure and organizational structure will map to one another without much redundancy or duplication.

Even with a redesigned organization, however, there may still be items that have no natural business owner. These items can be owned centrally, either by a corporate-level business unit or by a centralized IT department. There may also be duplications that cannot be resolved into a separately owned unit. These may be items that are too key to be surrendered by their owners, or items that look similar but prove to be not quite so similar on close inspection, or items that lend themselves to fine-grained reuse that is simply not cost-effective.

4.2.2 Change management

In the simplest case, it is in the owning business unit's interest to provide an application that others can use. For example, making an expenses or timesheet system available makes it easier for the accounts department to streamline the handling of expense requests or timesheets. A single customer management application makes it possible for the corporation to handle customer relationships in a unified and consistent way.

In these cases, change is naturally managed in one place only, by the owning business unit. Other business units will be prepared to accept changes as the owning business unit makes them (with acceptance testing to ensure that changes do not cause problems in interfaces with their own components).

In more complex cases, each business unit will have its own requirements, and will wish to negotiate its own changes, leading to change management issues. If each business unit legitimately wishes to operate differently, this may indicate that ownership has been misplaced. It may be that the application components over which there is dispute should be owned by individual business units rather than by the common application.

For instance, in the case of customer management some information is common, but some information about customers genuinely varies depending on the business unit. This business unit-specific information is best owned by the business unit rather than by the common application. A component-based approach facilitates this since the application can be carved up into smaller units – components – rather than being developed as a monolithic entity.

4.2.3 Using a common software solution versus reuse of components

The previous section indicates the importance of exactly how a component is reused. It is easier for everyone to use a common software solution when the software organization mirrors the corporate organization. A component-based approach makes it easier to achieve this, and it is then likely that many components will in fact occur in only one place in the overall application portfolio rather than being "reused". They are used more – because duplication is avoided.

An internal market becomes relevant when different business units use separate copies of the same application, maybe tailored to their specific needs, or use their own copy of a component. For instance, several business units may need to convert currencies for their own purposes. There is benefit in using the same software to do it, but no compelling reason why there should be a single application that carries out currency conversion. So each business unit might use its own applications, and include in them a component for currency conversion that is instantiated separately for that unit from any other instantiation in other applications.

The internal market model is also appropriate where an organization is not (yet?) so perfectly organized that its software structure can mirror its organizational one, desirable though such an organization is. It would be nice to think this was the exception rather than the rule.

4.3   The internal market model

Some form of internal market model within the organization often becomes relevant where there is a desire to reuse components across more than one business unit but no desire to design and use a common solution.

This section discusses the relevance of an internal market and provides a summary of the issues to be addressed by it. The summary is followed by two outlines of how an internal market could be created to enable collaboration across business units in the reuse of components.

4.3.1   Why is an internal market relevant?

The use of components by more than one business unit raises commercial issues. When I build a component for sale to other organizations, the commercial issues are self-evident. I will not be able to persuade a buyer to purchase my component if the buyer is not convinced it is good value for the money asked, that it is fit for the buyer's purposes, and that maintenance and support issues can be dealt with adequately.

However, a moment's thought makes it apparent that these same commercial issues arise within a single business organization. If I manage a business unit, the yardstick used to measure my success is likely to be the net income my business unit achieves. Given this, why should my group agree to delays in delivery dates and the higher cost involved in making a component reusable if the beneficiary will be another group, not my own? Obviously, if you want to interest me in this proposition, there would have to be some payback for my business unit.

Even assuming we can agree on collaboration, how should we manage the maintenance life cycle after first deployment? What happens when one business unit needs a change to the software? Won't the other business units refuse to implement the change, preferring to continue with the tried and tested software that is already in deployment rather than risking the deployment of a revised component that offers no improvements from their perspective?

These concerns, however, are no different from those that have to be addressed before the business unit will purchase software products from an external organization. Will I get a return on my investment that justifies the purchase? How does this affect my delivery dates? How is maintenance handled? Purchasing third-party products is usually regarded as a viable option, and this fact seems to me to adequately demonstrate that it is possible to find answers to the issues raised by the reuse of software across business units. Continuing along this line of thought, it seems as if cooperation will be possible if an internal market within the organization can be created that handles purchase and sale similarly to that of third-party products.

The *sale* of components (as opposed to their purchase) may still, however, be regarded by the business units as a distraction from their main business. With corporate approval, this role could be taken on by a central unit, maybe a unit within the IT department.

From the point of view of the individual business units, the same commercial issues apply to an internal market as to an external market. On the other hand, from the point of view of the organization, cooperation across business units might be to the greater good of the organization as a whole, either because consistency in approach across the organization brings benefits or because of potential cost savings.

We need to find ways of balancing the needs of the individual fiefdom with those of the larger whole. In order to achieve this balance, it is likely to be necessary to ensure that the balance sheets of the individual business units do in fact reflect their contribution to the common good.

4.3.2 Issues to be addressed by an internal market model

In summary, the issues to be addressed by an internal market model are:

- Who will pay for any extra development effort required to make a component usable outside the business unit that develops it?
- When changes are required, who will pay for them?
- How are changes rolled out? Must one business unit reimplement and retest an item of software because another business unit requires changes?

Two alternative ownership models are outlined below, with suggested ways of handling these issues.

4.3.2.1 Ownership by the business units

The owning business unit generally bears the cost of production of the component. It is often in the owning business unit's interest for other business units to use the component in order to ensure consistency of processing, so that no charge is made for use. Where the use is unrelated, a charge is likely to be made.

When a change is required that both (or all) business units need, a single version can be updated and put into production. If the change is one that one

business unit needs but another does not, a useful strategy is to put it into production for one business unit and to update the other business unit when that
unit next needs an update for its own reasons. In the long run costs will be kept
down for both business units if they agree to use the same component version
rather than developing divergent ones. (See Chapter 2 for comments on how
change can be handled.)

If the change is one that one business unit positively does not want, there will
be a relapse into using divergent software. The cost of this relapse should be
clearly spelt out, so that the parties can see whether allowing the software to
diverge will cost more than the perceived benefit is worth, or whether the
attempt to use a common component was in fact not cost-effective. It may be
possible to cut the component into a common part and divergent parts, to
reduce maintenance effort.

4.3.2.2 Ownership by a central unit

A central unit can combine two types of funding:

1 board-level funding, in which flat amounts are levied from the business units
for the development and management of reusable assets and components;

2 self-funding, in which the central unit takes a business risk on the costs and
revenues of the components it manages. This means it is entitled to supply a
component at a price that is based on its own estimate of the potential
number of purchasers.

Funding via a flat-rate levy has the advantage that it makes it possible to supply
components cheaply or even without charge. This provides individual projects
with strong incentives to use the common assets, since doing so reduces their
overall cost, thus improving the overall level of reuse.

Where assets from a central unit are used, questions are often raised about the
management of change, and the inconvenience of one business unit being
affected by changes required by another business unit. The best solution to this
is to use the same maintenance model for centrally managed assets as for bought
software, since business units are, after all, willing to accept this model for
bought software.

To give a brief outline of the approach:

1 The central unit sets the price for supplying a component. There is likely to
be an upfront cost and an ongoing charge for maintenance.

2 The central unit bears the cost of maintaining the software, in line with
service agreements.

3 Business units can choose to take updated versions of the software or not, but
old versions will not be supported indefinitely. Business units must accept the
cost of retesting software when they incorporate new component versions.

This approach is similar to, but slightly more formal than, the one proposed for
use where components are owned by business units.

5 Software architecture and infrastructure

Software architecture is about how we set about bringing parts together to form a whole system. An architecture comprises the set of rules, guidelines, and conventions used to define the structure of a system in terms of its component parts. It defines how the parts of that system communicate and interoperate.

A builder has the advantage of being able to use a known repertory of types of brick, that may be in different sizes and made of different materials. For software, there is no predefined list that defines the types of component we can use. Consequently we must define our own repertory of component types, as well as architectural templates that explain how we might use these.

Chapter 2 explained the need for a supporting environment for components. If we want components that are (relatively) context-independent, a standard (architected) approach to component interaction is needed. An architected approach is also needed if our components are to fit together in terms of their content. Components and an architected approach to software development thus go hand-in-hand. The use of an architected approach, which is necessary for components, is of course desirable in its own right.

Consequently, one of the planning activities required for a component-based approach is the definition of a strategy for software architecture and infrastructure, and it is this chapter's objective to consider the various aspects that an architecture for CBD needs to cover.

5.1 Areas of architectural concern

Architectural concerns can be split between those relating to the software infrastructure and those relating to the components that operate within that infrastructure.

As we develop and evolve our architecture, functionality has a tendency to move down into the software infrastructure or supporting environment. This makes it easier to achieve the objective of making component interaction context-independent. It also makes it possible for components to concentrate on business logic while technical issues are handled within the software infrastructure. Software infrastructures for components can be acquired in the form of component execution environments such as EJB. These handle some but not all of what can be addressed by the software infrastructure. The remaining requirements must usually be met through development of an in-house software infrastructure, although there may be some aspects that are formalized into component frameworks which are available as third-party products.

Given this natural split between business-level components and software infrastructure, we can divide architectural concerns into two separate parts:

1 the technical architecture, which defines both the technical environment and the software infrastructure;

2 the application architecture, which covers the architectural issues faced by component developers and assemblers.

Figure 5.1 shows schematically these two areas of concern.

5.1.1 Technical architecture

The technical architecture is shown in Figure 5.1 as including two areas:

● the technical environment, which includes the component execution environment, operating system, and hardware platform;

● the software infrastructure, or component framework.

5.1.1.1 Technical environment

In most technical environments these days, more than one machine is involved (and usually also more than one type of hardware platform), and there is some

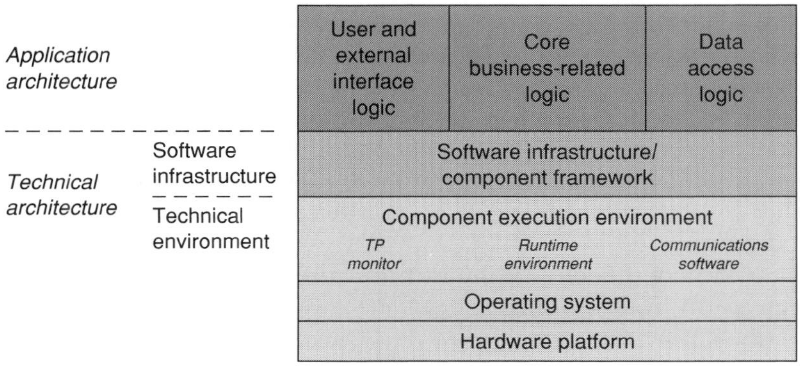

Figure 5.1
Application architecture and technical architecture

level of use of distributed applications. User access may be PC-based, using either a browser-based interface or a GUI (graphical user interface). Alternatively, or in addition, access to applications may be possible via other types of external interface, such as business-to-business communications, e-mail, telephone, fax, WAP, etc. Where new application software is required, it is often developed for a middle tier, which is frequently Unix-based, while existing back-end systems are often hosted by a wide variety of platforms, running operating systems such as MVS or VMS.

So defining the technical environment involves defining:

- the hardware platforms to be used and their operating systems;
- the technologies to be used, e.g. TP monitor, programing languages, communications software. These technologies may be bundled into a component execution environment, or dictated by it.

It is also necessary to consider how components built using the different technologies, to run on different platforms, can interoperate reasonably transparently, i.e. with as little awareness as possible on the part of one component of the technical characteristics of another component. To achieve this, technical dependencies must be isolated and the way the component presents itself to its environment standardized.

Some of these aspects can be handled through the definition of the technical environment, e.g. through a decision to use COM or CORBA or Java-only technology. The software infrastructure is responsible for any other aspects that are required in order to achieve components that are context-independent.

5.1.1.2 *Software infrastructure*

Software infrastructure is required in order to provide a supporting environment for components. It is also desirable as a matter of good software engineering practice, regardless of the use of components, to develop and evolve a software infrastructure, to promote consistency and reduce effort.

A software infrastructure is used to incorporate those parts of an application that can be standardized. For instance, a standard user interface style could be used. Without standardization, development effort is repeated by the application developer each time an application is developed. Standardization makes it feasible to remove code that would otherwise be coded by hand, as part of the business-oriented components, into a separate, reusable software infrastructure. This reduces development effort and simplifies the application developer's task. The software infrastructure can be provided in the form of a pre-built component *framework* that handles standardized aspects of component behavior, together possibly with code generators that generate parts of the application in a standard way.

The services of the software infrastructure may be partly supplied by system software, partly by off-the-shelf software frameworks, and partly by custom-built software and generators.

5.1.2 Application architecture

The technical architecture handles aspects that are often common across a number of applications. The application architecture, on the other hand, is concerned with the application logic that is needed for specific applications. In order to create an application architecture, it is necessary to have a picking list of component types and a definition of how components of these different types can interact. This can be called a *component model*.

Standardization of the expected size and shape of components increases the probability that two components developed independently (e.g. for two different applications or by two different vendors) could be brought together into a single application. This definition of component types is like defining the types of building block to be used in a building.

If you adopt a standard component model, this will cover at least a part of what is required. It is still desirable to add rules and guidelines on top of those provided by a standard component model. In addition, you need a *business component model*, or *component blueprint*. This defines the set of components that meets a business's specific needs. It could, for instance, cover order processing or the management of bank accounts. It seems logical to believe that you could define a reasonably standard set of types of component that could be used for applications for a wide variety of business domains.

Business component models, on the other hand, are specific to a particular business domain. It would be possible to develop a standard business component model for a single business domain, e.g. stocks and shares. In fact, some standard business models have been available for years and there are ongoing efforts, as mentioned in Chapter 2, to standardize business concepts in a wide variety of business domains. Packaged software, of course, incorporates a business model, which could (or must) be adopted "as-is" by an organization that uses the package. Generally, though, an organization is interested in components because business needs mean that applications should be tailored to an organization's specific needs. Consequently, it will be necessary for an organization either to build its own component blueprint or to tailor a standard business component model to its needs.

Figure 5.1 shows the software infrastructure as part of the technical architecture. However, it is an area that protrudes into the area of concern of application architects because, while the technical architecture could provide a full software infrastructure, partly bought and partly custom-built, a variable-sized portion of the activity of building the software infrastructure is commonly left to the component developers and assemblers. In fact, what usually happens over time is that application developers come to recognize parts of their work as repetitive and therefore start to develop software infrastructures to handle these. As a result, areas that were the concern of the application developer move down into the software infrastructure.

The software infrastructure can be treated as a domain in its own right, with its own development team. Alternatively, the standardized parts of the software infrastructure may be the responsibility of the technical architecture group.

5.2   Technical environment issues

It is an objective for componentware that components should interoperate transparently. For this to be possible, all components must look the same to other components. They must behave uniformly, which could be achieved if they all conformed to a single standard. This presents enormous challenges at the present time, however, both because of the variety of platforms in use and the fact that we must cater for existing applications that require component façades.

To what extent do existing component models enable transparent interoperation across platforms? Microsoft's COM does not cover all platforms, while EJB is a server-side model that is Java-only. J2EE (Java 2 Platform, Enterprise Edition) includes EJB and aims to cover the design of multi-tier enterprise applications using Java. J2EE is still limited to Java, but it includes a draft J2EE Connector Architecture that defines a standard API for connecting to non-Java applications. The Connector Architecture defines quite a low-level interface and it seems as if further time will be necessary before it is possible to have a uniform view of components across platforms.[1]

One disadvantage of Java is that it runs inside its own virtual machine. This means that you cannot mix Java and non-Java code within a single process. If you want to put a component façade on existing applications that are not written in Java, it is easier to do this using a language such as C or C++, which can inhabit the same process as your existing application. For this reason, CORBA and CCM remain relevant for legacy integration, even if you expect to do most new application development in Java.

5.2.1   A vision of interoperable components

While there are limits at present to the extent to which transparent interoperation of components across platforms is feasible, it is worth considering what would be needed to make it possible for components to interoperate across technologies. We would need:

● a common interface technology that implements messaging and allows components written in different languages for different operating systems and hardware to interact with one another;

● common component behavior across environments, so that components do not have to know what technology was used to build the components whose services they use.

1. Despite its gestures in the direction of application integration, it seems as if the EJB specification was the product of an earlier era in which we could still think of new development as an isolated activity, instead of thinking from the outset that any new application is likely to be put together by integrating existing software. Thus EJB operates as a sandbox and does not address how EJB-based applications communicate with non-EJB-based ones. This is doubtless due for correction over time as J2EE and subsequent developments emerge.

While the need for common interface technology is well understood, since it applies whether or not a component-based approach is adopted, the need for common component behavior is less often appreciated. As already indicated, definitions of component behavior are emerging from, for instance, the OMG's work on components, Model Driven Architecture and CORBA, Microsoft's .NET and COM, the J2EE/EJB specification, and earlier work by IBM on its Component Broker and on San Francisco. Takeup of EJB and COM is good, with CORBA in increasing use in its own right and as an underpinning for higher-level models such as EJB or CCM. But these component models are still developing and it is necessary to provide bridges between the different component models and with components that use other technologies.

Figure 5.2 shows a simplified view of the way components interact and the services they require.

5.2.1.1 Component execution environment

We can assume that each component operates in the context of a component execution environment, e.g. EJB or an environment that has been defined in-house. In Figure 5.2, the dependency of a component on its environment is shown by embedding the component in the environment. A component can be said to plug into its supporting component execution environment, which provides a socket for it. There are usually services offered by the component execution environment that the component invokes explicitly. In addition, when a component is invoked, or invokes a service in another component, the request will normally be handled by the component execution environment. This enables the component execution environment to add logic – for example, logic that enables it to handle transactions implicitly, without it being necessary for the component itself to be explicitly involved in commit and rollback decisions. The fact that a component

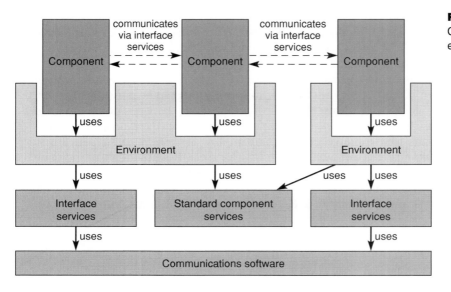

Figure 5.2
Component execution environment

uses the interfaces of the component execution environment and relies on its implicit capabilities does, of course, couple the component to a specific component execution environment, or at least to an environment that implements the same component model or the same capabilities.

The environment determines the capabilities of the component. While ideally all components would be capable of offering similar behavior, in practice there will be differences. For instance, some components may be capable of peer-to-peer behavior, while others are implemented using a technology that makes only master–slave relationships possible.

The capabilities offered by the environment also affect the technical details of how components can achieve an interface with components in other environments, for example what protocols can be used.

Figure 5.2 also illustrates the concept of a "container" as it shows two separate "environment" containers. These two containers could be implemented using the same component model, for instance EJB, or one container could be an EJB container while the other could be a CORBA, CCM, or COM container.

5.2.1.2   *Communications software and interface services*

Components may need to communicate with components in the same environment or with those in another environment. This should be done in a standard way – the component should not need to be coded differently depending on whether a component it uses is in the same or a different environment.

Different technologies offer different interfacing capabilities. It is desirable to abstract away from this diversity, so that components adopt a standard approach to communications and remain unaware of technology-dependent differences in these.

A current obstacle in the way of this vision is the reality of multiple communications standards, for instance, COM, CORBA, and RMI.[2] While applications can be built to use more than one communications standard, there is still an impact for the component developer. For instance, a transaction cannot involve both COM and CORBA-based communications. RMI can operate over IIOP, which means that it uses the CORBA message format. The EJB specification defines an interoperability protocol that is based on CORBA/IIOP. It also recommends that security and transaction context should be passed using the CORBA standard mechanisms, to enable interoperability between different vendors' EJB containers and between CORBA applications and EJB enterprise beans. This means that there is greater compatibility between CORBA and EJB, so that CORBA clients can include both CORBA and EJB components in the same transaction. On the other hand, the ability of an EJB component to act as a client for a CORBA component depends on the capabilities provided by any specific EJB server implementation, and is not defined in the EJB standard.

---

2. RMI (Remote Method Invocation) is the Java version of what is generally known as a remote procedure call, but with the ability to pass one or more objects along with the request.

5.2.1.3   Standard component services

In order to standardize the behavior of components developed using different technologies, standard component services can be used. Shown in Figure 5.2, these:

- are software infrastructure services specifically intended for use in a component-oriented environment;
- reduce the complexity of developing components by enabling common types of logic to be handled by the standard component services instead of by code within the component itself;
- ensure that components handle certain software issues such as service location, user authorization, transaction management, thread management, event notification, garbage collection, etc. in a standard way;
- can be implemented as a component framework.

Different versions of these standard services could be implemented by each component execution environment, to meet its own needs and constraints. Even within one component execution environment, there could be multiple implementations of the services, with individual implementations that are specific to a particular context (e.g. Internet), or even to the needs of a particular type of component. Some services, however, should be shared between component execution environments. For instance, transaction management must be shared in order to enable two-phase commit of transactions across container boundaries. Where environments really can interoperate successfully, one environment could use standard services implemented using another environment.

Using standard component services across multiple environments, as shown in Figure 5.2, makes it easier for components developed using different technologies to interoperate. It does, however, depend on multiple environment vendors agreeing to use common standards. The nearest approach to a common standard for component services available today is the standard for CORBA services, and it is no doubt for this reason that the use of some of these services is leveraged in the EJB specification.

The following are some of the most widely useful services.

- Location services. These services are used by one component or piece of software to obtain the location of a service it requires. Using a location service to do this means that the location of components can be changed freely without having to revise the calling code. It also makes it possible to add capabilities such as load balancing, so that a request can be directed to alternative copies of a component, and failover, so if one component or the platform it is on fails, requests can be redirected to another version of the component. Examples of standards for location services are:

  — JNDI (Java Naming and Directory Interface). This interface can sit on top of other location services, such as the CORBA COS Naming Service and the LDAP directory interface.

— CORBA's Naming Service. This service is analogous to a telephone book's white pages. You can find a service provided you know its name.

— CORBA's Trader Service. The Trader Service is a more flexible version of the Naming Service that is analogous to a telephone book's yellow pages. You can select from a number of providers of a service based on the advertised properties of the service.

● Transaction management. Here, EJB uses the Java language version of the CORBA Transaction Service, which is additionally available in other languages such as C++. It wraps the JTS with an API (the JTA – Java Transaction API). This makes it possible for an EJB server vendor to use the JTA to wrap transaction management technologies other than the JTS, although transactional interoperability between EJB containers from different vendors depends on both vendors using the JTS.

Transaction management across multiple technologies and component models is a non-trivial issue and some of the issues are discussed later in this chapter.

● Security. Security services can address a range of topics, in particular:

— authentication – checking the identity of a user or piece of executing software;

— authorization – determining which services a user or piece of software should be allowed to use;

— security of communications – ensuring that client and target components can trust each other's identity and that communications cannot be snooped on or tampered with;

— non-repudiation – providing irrefutable evidence that an action has taken place to protect against subsequent attempts to deny that data was received or sent.

The CORBA Security Service provides one specification for security-related services and, as mentioned previously, EJB relies on the security context being propagated as part of an IIOP message, in accordance with the CORBA standard. Another relevant standard is the Java™ Authentication and Authorization Service (JAAS), which addresses the issue of standardizing user authentication for Java applications.

● Events, notifications, and messaging. This category of service addresses the need for asynchronous communications (messaging) and, over and above this, the need for decoupled, asynchronous communications between event suppliers and event consumers. Whereas simple point-to-point asynchronous messaging simply directs a message to a single known consumer, without requiring a synchronous response, more complex publish–subscribe event-handling models make it possible for there to be multiple suppliers and consumers of a single type of event, and also make it possible for a component to issue an event without knowing which, if any, consumers there are for an event. This decoupling of supplier and consumer is ideal for components, since it means that a component can be developed without knowledge of how it will be used and without a requirement for code change when components are added that require knowledge of the events or notifications it issues. Examples of this type of capability are:

— the Java Messaging Service (JMS), which is used for message-driven beans in the EJB 2.0 specification and covers both point-to-point and publish–subscribe mechanisms;

— the CORBA Event Service, the CORBA Notification Service (which is a version of the Event Service with added capabilities, e.g. for event filtering), and the CORBA Messaging Service.

While the above standard services are likely to be included in a standard component execution environment, based for instance on EJB or CCM, there are likely to be further aspects of the software infrastructure that can usefully be standardized but are not provided as part of the component execution environment. For instance, a logging service could be a useful addition, that could be provided as part of an organization's own software infrastructure.

5.2.2   Component interoperation in practice

The ideal situation for component-based software would be one in which there was a single standard for interface services, and all environments offered the same capabilities using a set of standard component services that shared common definitions. Given current technology, however, the technology used to implement a component will not be fully transparent. Components implemented using different technologies will have different characteristics.

One of the tasks of the technical architecture is to mitigate this problem. This can be done through a combination of strategies:

● selection of a restricted range of technologies for use, so as to reduce technical incompatibilities and inconsistencies;

● isolation of technology-specific aspects, so that components can be made relatively technology-neutral;

● acceptance of constraints on how some or all components can interact, e.g. whether transactions can cross component boundaries or not.

Technology-dependent aspects are best handled in a way that has as good a potential for upward compatibility as can be reasonably achieved without second-guessing future developments. It rarely pays to delay any development more than a few weeks in order to wait for technology improvements that technology vendors are claiming will appear soon.

5.2.2.1   *Transaction management*

Managing transactions that cross component boundaries is most easily achieved where all three of the following apply:

● the same database is used for all the updates required in a transaction;

- the components participating in the transaction are all on the same host;
- the same component execution environment is used by all the components.

In such a case, the start and commit boundaries of the transaction can be included in one of the components or can be handled by the component execution environment. To take an example of how a component execution environment can handle a transaction, EJB allows the application assembler to specify that transaction support is "Required" for a bean. In this case, if the bean is invoked in a context in which a transaction is already established, it participates in the transaction that is already open. If no transaction has been established yet, the component execution environment starts one.

Making the component execution environment responsible for transaction management is more flexible than leaving this responsibility in components, because it means that a component that, when it is first used, starts and ends a transaction can later be incorporated in a larger transaction without any requirement for code change.

More complicated issues arise where any of the following apply to the transaction.

- Heterogeneous databases – the data involved is stored in more than one database, maybe from different database vendors.
- Distributed databases – the data involved is stored in databases at physically separate locations, managed by physically separate processors.
- Nested transactions – one or more of the business components is a legacy component that includes commit statements. A new application requires a new database transaction that has to include the existing transaction(s) as nested transaction(s) that can be rolled back if the overall transaction fails.
- Multi-process transactions – the business components are implemented as separately executable processes that cannot share the same database connection.

There are technological solutions for some of these cases. Table 5.1 shows technologies that provide some possible solutions.

Of course, these technologies only provide solutions if they can be used with the technologies that implement the components. Where a component provides a façade for a legacy application, it is unlikely to be possible for the legacy application to participate in a distributed transaction across heterogeneous technologies unless the database access code is revised or rewritten, and quite possibly not even then.

For this reason, transactions that cross heterogeneous technologies are usually still avoided. However, as databases increasingly provide XA[3] interfaces in both Java and C++, and as EJB Servers and CORBA products increasingly make CORBA Transaction Services available, it is to be expected that the use of transactions that cross technology boundaries will increase.

---

3. An industry standard based on the X/Open CAE Specification (Distributed Transaction Processing: the XA Specification). The XA interface defines the contract between a Resource Manager and a Transaction Manager in a distributed transaction processing (DTP) environment.

Table 5.1 Technological solutions for some transactions problems

Problem	Technologies and standards
Heterogeneous databases	Middleware such as *Microsoft Transaction Server* *BEA's TUXEDO* *IBM's ENCINA* *CORBA Transaction Services* *EJB Servers' Java Transaction Services* Relevant standards include: *Open Group's X/OPEN XATMI* *OMG's CORBA Transaction Service* *Sun's Java Transaction Service*
Distributed databases	A number of database management systems (DBMSs) support distributed database transactions, for example Oracle
Nested transactions	Supported by some DBMSs
Multi-process transactions	There are often ways of allowing processes to share a database connection, either through the DBMS or through middleware products that support transaction processing for heterogeneous databases

5.2.2.2   *Legacy software*

Even when technology for components is better developed, it will still be a requirement that component-based applications can include legacy software that was not built for interoperability.

If we simply invoke legacy software directly from components, component software must be aware that it is not dealing with a component that behaves in a standard way. To make it possible for components to interface with other components in a uniform way, unaware of whether the software is legacy software or not, the legacy software must be packaged, or wrapped, within a containing component that conforms to standards. Such wrapping makes it more possible for other components to interact with components that wrap legacy code without being affected by the limitations of the legacy code.

In addition, the use of wrapping means that when the legacy code is replaced, the impact of the change is limited, as the new component presents the same interface as the replaced wrapped legacy component.

5.3   Software infrastructure issues

As already discussed, much of the software infrastructure may be predetermined, and supplied, as a result of the selection of a specific component execution environment. The remaining definition task involves filling in the gaps and determining how much of the development task can be handled in a standard way.

It may be necessary to define standard component services that are not offered as part of the component execution environment. For all services, whether offered as standard by the component execution environment or added as part of a company-specific software infrastructure, guidelines for use are often desirable to ensure that all developers adopt a uniform approach.

Examples of standard capabilities that could be supported by the software infrastructure are:

- workflow (discussed in the next section);
- the standard services already covered in Section 5.2.1.3 on page 59, if not covered by the component execution environment;
- standard ways of handling relationships between objects, for instance "Order placed by Customer";
- a standard for declaring the interface of an operation;
- management of data storage;
- failover, load balancing, and recovery;
- logging and error handling.

In addition there are some software infrastructure issues that are not significantly affected by the use of components. For instance:

- definition of standards for user interface style and user interface logic and the possible use of productivity tools for speeding the development of user interfaces that conform to these standards;
- similarly, standardization of data access logic.

The simplest approach to providing standard capabilities is to define development standards to which developers must adhere.

Further options are to use pre-built code (either frameworks or callable routines) to cover parts of the required logic. For instance, an OO framework could be used for user interface code. Templates and generators can be provided to help to produce code in a standardized way and to add standard logic to components.

In addition, as component assembly environments emerge, components will be required to provide enquiry services that the assembly environment can invoke to enable it to provide intelligent assistance to software developers who are assembling components, similar to the mechanisms used in JavaBeans. The format of these will depend on the assembly environment.

5.3.1 Workflow

Business processes often involve sequences of activities where one participant carries out a task and then may pass documents and information to other participants so that they can carry out subsequent tasks. Parts of these sequences may be automated, carried out by a computer with or without human involvement, while some may be carried out wholly manually.

Computer systems often provide support for individual activities within a business process, but do not put these together or dictate the sequence in which activities are carried out. Instead, the people involved in carrying out the business process determine the order in which tasks should be carried out, and by whom.

With workflow systems, however, explicit support is provided for managing the flow of activities. These systems are provided with a workflow definition on which they can manage the flow of activities and the allocation of tasks to suitable resources, whether these are human or machine. The term *workflow* is sometimes used to refer to the computerized facilitation or automation of a process, where it may well be the case that computer assistance is available for only part of a process.[4]

Where workflow automation is part of a company's objectives, the company's architecture definition needs to include a management infrastructure that manages workflows, including the handling of worklists, the starting, stopping and controlling of process instances, and the navigation between the activities in a process.

5.4 Application architecture issues

As stated previously, the application architecture is concerned with the application logic that is needed for specific applications. In order to create an application architecture, it is necessary to define:

- a *component model* – this provides a picking list of component types and a definition of how components of these different types can interact;
- a *business component model* or *component blueprint* – this defines the set of components that meets a business's specific needs. Note that while business components (as defined in the next chapter) form the core of this model, the component blueprint should also cover the other types of component that are needed.

This section considers some of the principles that are important when defining a good application architecture, in particular the use of domains and layers. Chapter 6 outlines a specific layered architecture in more detail.

5.4.1 Separability and the definition of architectural domains

The importance of separability as a defining feature of components was discussed in Chapter 2. Separability enables us to limit the extent to which any component is impacted by change or replacement of another component or by its use in a new context.

---

4. See the Workflow Management Coalition's Workflow Reference Model for a definition of workflow. See www.wfmc.org for more information.

This same principle is also applicable when defining an application architecture and can be applied by dividing up applications into domains, where a domain is a separately identifiable area that can be considered in its own right and is coded separately.

A core set of three domains was shown in Figure 5.1 on page 53:

- presentation – responsible for user interface and external interface logic;
- business logic – responsible for core business-related logic;
- data access – responsible for reading and updating data held in storage.

The rationale for separating logic into domains is that it eases reuse.

One example of this from my experience is a call center application which was built as a standalone application using Oracle and Oracle's stored procedures. It was originally expected to deal primarily with new customers (prospects) rather than existing ones. Once it was in operation, it was decided that the application should additionally access the central customer database, which used a different database system on a different platform, to find out whether a caller was already a customer or not. When we examined the application, we found that the business logic and the data access logic were inextricably mingled in the stored procedures, so that the business logic could not be used with a different database. We could only connect to the customer database by writing new modules that duplicated the business logic from the stored procedures, separating it from the data access logic, so that the business logic could be used with a different database. If the original application had cleanly separated business logic and data access logic, our task would have been much easier.

Similar examples occur all the time with user interface logic, as the way we interact with applications changes. Applications that originally used green screens required revision so that a PC-based GUI could be used. Today, browser-based interfaces are required as applications become web-based. Additional alternative methods of access are liable to become necessary, including:

- automated access to applications by customers using a phone line, for instance to operate a bank account;
- extension of this automated access to the use of WAP or SMS;
- automated handling of faxes, letters, and e-mail;
- business-to-business communications via file, EDI, or over the Internet.

As these examples demonstrate, separating business logic from presentation logic and from data access logic will help make applications more maintainable.

Common services are also usefully separated out. Ultimately, these may become part of the software infrastructure if they are applicable to more than one application.

It is best to design in a way so that each component that could potentially be delivered separately belongs to a single domain. This makes it possible to replace the data access element, for instance, or to use the same presentation component with a different business logic implementation. This approach also eases distribution. Each component at this level of granularity can reasonably be either co-located or distributed, and packaging each such component separately means that the decision to co-locate or to distribute can be a deployment one.[5]

On the other hand, a decision could be made that a certain set of components will always be deployed together and that they should therefore be packaged as a component assembly. In this case, distribution decisions can be taken before the installation package is built, and the component assembly will fix the options that it allows – for instance, which data storage alternatives it caters for.

5.4.2   Interactions between components in different domains

In addition, it is useful to standardize the way that components in each of the domains interact with each other. The most common approach is to define a layered architecture.

The basic principle of a layered architecture is that in each layer all the components play a similar client role with respect to components in the layer below, and a server role with respect to components in the layer above. Figure 5.3 illustrates this principle.

The fact that requests are made in a single direction helps reduce dependencies between components. Thus, while a component in the presentation layer requires the presence of any business logic layer component it uses, the business logic layer component is not dependent on the presence of any presentation layer component and can be used in any number of contexts with different presentation layer components. (You may, of course, choose to reuse the presentation layer components but you are not obliged to.) Similarly, the business logic components require data access components that present certain defined interfaces, but the data access components require no knowledge of the business logic components.

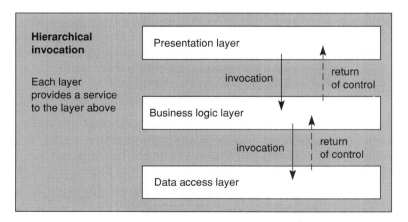

Figure 5.3
Principles of a layered architecture

5. This is not quite true where a component requires a proxy on another platform when it is distributed. In this case, the proxy requires separate installation. Proxies are discussed further in Chapter 6.

The use of layers provides a simple way to control interdependencies and to ensure that no component in one layer will be dependent on any component in its client layer.

5.4.3 Optionality of the layers

One issue that has to be resolved with respect to a layered architecture is the optionality of the layers. Can a component in one layer be omitted, and components allowed to communicate directly across more than one layer, or must components always be present in all layers?

An architecture is described as *open* if a component in one layer can interact with a component in a layer not immediately adjacent to it, and *closed* if components may interact only with immediately adjacent components.

A closed architecture is simpler but may result in components in one layer that do nothing other than pass calls on to another layer, which is not desirable. An architecture must define a standard solution that indicates which layers may be bypassed and which may not. Where layers can be bypassed, so that one layer may invoke components in more than one other layer, it is important that the alternative layers should present the same interface. This is necessary so that when a need for the missing layer is identified, it can be added without having a knock-on effect on all clients.

5.4.4 Use of events for controlled peer-to-peer communications

The use of events provides a way of relaxing the rule that a component can only communicate down the layers, not up, and does so without creating additional dependencies.

Generally, in an OO architecture objects are thought of as independent entities, which are "equal" and can communicate peer-to-peer. Objects can be seen as implementing concurrent processes. This model has some relevance to distributed processing and offers greater flexibility for the definition of components. Its disadvantage is the greater complexity of the model and the potential for complex interdependencies between objects (the OO version of spaghetti code).

The potential complexity can be reduced by implementing a layered architecture but with some relaxations as follows.

1 Peer-to-peer communications are usually allowed within a layer. Thus business object A could invoke an operation X in business object B, which could then invoke operation Y in business object A.

2 Within and between layers, events can be used to allow an object to communicate in the opposite direction to that specified by the layers (i.e. server to client). An event notification mechanism makes it possible to do this while preserving the independence of the server component from client components.

Figure 5.4 illustrates the use of peer-to-peer communications *within* a layer.

The event notification mechanism allows peer-to-peer communication *without* creating additional dependencies. It works, in brief, as follows. In this example, I refer to user interface and business objects to make the example more concrete, but the use of event notification is not restricted to these two types of object.

- A user interface object sends a message to a business object to register an interest in events that affect that business object (i.e. cause its internal state to change). In this case, the user interface object is the *event subscriber*.

- The business object records the identity of the interested subscriber object. To do this, it records only the subscriber object's object reference. It requires no other knowledge of the subscriber object, not even its type. This is the key point that makes the business object completely independent of the subscriber objects. The business object is the *event publisher*.

- When an event affects the business object, it notifies all objects that have registered an interest in that event (it *publishes* the event).

Figure 5.5 shows how this mechanism operates.

This approach can be used, for instance, to make it possible for a number of windows that are showing the same business object to reflect that update as soon as it is made. For instance, if you move a file all directory windows that are open on your desktop could be updated immediately to show the new position of the file without requiring you to refresh each window.

How does the event notification mechanism ensure that components are just as independent of one another as with the strict layered approach? The key point is that the *event publisher* object is kept independent of all *subscriber* objects. This is achieved through the fact that all objects have a common style of object identification and are programed using an identical set of constructs. All objects look the same. The only thing the event publisher knows about the

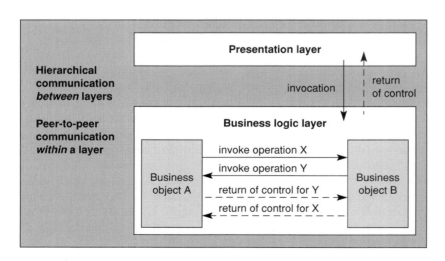

Figure 5.4
Peer-to-peer communication within a layer

Figure 5.5
Example of event
notification

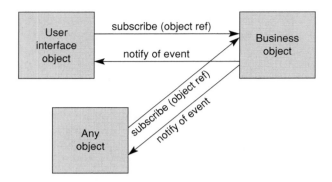

subscriber is its object reference. No part of the event publisher's code has to be tailored to cater for any particular types of subscriber. Because of this, the business object can be used in any context without any necessity for the user interface objects to be present as well.

Allowing peer-to-peer communications within a layer, and using event notification, does add complexity and it is best to use it only when the additional flexibility it gives is needed.

Events can be used *within* a component, but it is their potential use *between* components that is of particular interest to us. A component can be designed to publish events when certain changes occur to its own state. Other components can register an interest in these events without this introducing close coupling between the components – assuming, of course, a careful and logical definition of the events that are to be published.

5.4.5 Use of layers in practice

In practice, the use of layers often meets with resistance. This is partly because it requires more effort to separate logic into layers. It is much easier to start with the user interface and simply mix business logic into it. Without practical experience, it often seems difficult to work out where the two should be separated.

People often argue that the urgency of the development counterweighs the argument that separating concerns into different domains will make change easier later. They argue that there is no time for an architected approach. They may also argue that technology choices will not change.It is also common to be asked what processing is left when both the user interface logic and the data access logic are removed. A common view is that no logic will be left, since all that is involved in an application is the collection of data through the user interface and the storage of that in a database – there is no business logic.

But even the simplest application usually does have some business logic – orders are rejected if an item has been discontinued, for instance. If this logic is put either in the user interface or in the data access layers, it cannot be reused in different contexts and it cannot be modified in one place and one place only when it changes.

There may well be non-strategic applications that need to be developed in a quick and dirty fashion, and that will also be replaced quickly enough for their lack of maintainability not to be a problem. Alternatively, though, it can be argued that a development group that understands how to develop well-architected applications will be able to develop a well- (or at least well-enough) architected solution just as quickly as an unmaintainable one.

6 Defining components

This chapter considers what principles should govern how components are defined. It considers the types of component to use and how components of these types can be fitted together. It also considers the question of component scope. How large should a component be and what criteria can we use in order to decide the scope it should have?

To illustrate these principles, I outline a candidate set of component types, and make suggestions as to how to define components of these types. Obviously, I think this is a useful set of component types that will fit in with available technologies, but component models are evolving and any organization should choose its own set of component types to fit in with the model it uses and its own architectural requirements.

Component types should be defined within an overall application architecture which:

- identifies a number of software domains;
- specifies how these domains interrelate (e.g. as layers);
- defines standard rules to govern the relationships between software components in the different domains.

6.1 A layered architecture

This section describes how an application can be layered. These layers are very widely known and accepted, but there are differences in interpretation so that the view I present here is unlikely to be universally accepted in its finer details.

Figure 6.1 illustrates the simplest division into three distinct layers. These layers can be further subdivided, as I will explain.

6.1.1 Business logic layer

The business logic layer contains the core business-related logic that represents what the end user would regard as the subject matter of the system. For instance, it might handle the actions of debiting and crediting a bank account. It has the responsibility for ensuring that business rules are observed. To continue the example, if an account cannot be allowed to go into debit, it must ensure that this cannot happen. It is responsible for ensuring the integrity of corporate business data, so that data is consistent and only permitted updates are carried out. In order to achieve this, responsibility for transactions affecting corporate data must ultimately lie with the business logic layer.

Because it handles business logic, it is also responsible for business processes, to the extent that these are made explicit in the software.

It is useful to think of the business logic layer as representing primarily the *corporate* view. It represents the interests of the enterprise or organization rather than those of any client interacting with the organization or any agent acting on the organization's behalf.

We can also distinguish, as an area of secondary interest within the business logic layer, the representation of *departmental* views. There is a common core of logic and data that represents the corporate view. Around this common core, there are business processes that may belong to different departments within the organization. These may have their own specific data requirements and their own ways of looking at common data. For instance, the point of view of the accounts department tends to be different from that of human resources.

Whether workflow is used or not, the business logic layer naturally divides into:

- a layer that handles control logic, providing workflow support for business processes to a greater or lesser extent;

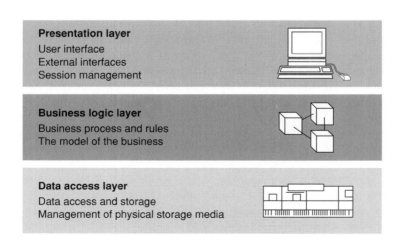

Presentation layer
User interface
External interfaces
Session management

Business logic layer
Business process and rules
The model of the business

Data access layer
Data access and storage
Management of physical storage media

Figure 6.1
A layered architecture

● a business object layer, in which the business domain is modeled in terms of the business objects included in it.

Conceptually, all requests that come into the business logic layer from the presentation or data access layer come in at the control layer. I say "conceptually" because requests could bypass the control layer – the real requirement is that if I do bypass the control layer, the architecture is such that I can readily insert control logic in front of the business object request when I need to, without having to change existing logic.

I said that requests from the data access layer should come in at the control layer. One case that can raise issues is when requests to the data access layer can result in asynchronous responses. These asynchronous events could be new business events that should come into the control layer, or they could be responses that should be handled by the business component that made the data access request, just as synchronous requests simply return control to the caller.

6.1.2 Presentation layer

The presentation layer:

● handles the presentation of information to users and the mechanisms that allow users to interact with the system, e.g. specific windows to allow entry of customer information, pushbuttons, list boxes, messages, etc;

● handles the user interface events that trigger processing in the business logic layer;

● manages other incoming and outgoing interfaces with external systems, e.g. incoming data feeds and outbound transmission of statutory information;

● handles the production of reports and the processing of batch files.

As a sublayer of the presentation layer, there may be a coordination or mapping layer that translates physical user input actions into the requests that the business logic layer understands.

The value of the presentation layer is that it isolates the business logic layer from the question of how a stimulus is received. A request coming into the business logic layer should look the same to it regardless of whether it is received as a result of human interaction with a user interface (whether GUI, browser, or PDA) or is triggered by an e-mail, a business-to-business communication, receipt of a file, or some time-related or business event.

Another function of the presentation layer is that, while the business logic layer looks after the interests of the enterprise, the presentation layer is concerned with the interests of the client or agent and is responsible for providing any aids that assist interaction with the application, including retention of information such as session data, user preferences, etc.

Often, such aids are dependent on the way in which the interaction is handled. Navigation between screens is required for a user interface, but not for messages between businesses. The style of screen handling varies depending on whether the user interface is a PDA, a mobile phone, a browser, or a GUI. This means that what you could regard as application logic forms a natural part of the presentation layer.

It can sometimes be tricky to separate application logic that belongs with the presentation layer from aspects that belong intrinsically to the management of the business logic. It may not always be readily apparent whether a particular processing flow simply seems appropriate because it works well with a given type of external interface, or whether the processing flow must necessarily happen in a particular way if the corporate business is to be handled correctly.

However, if these are separated successfully it will be possible to handle adding a new interface type at a later stage much more efficiently than could otherwise be done. A good test of the separation is to consider how easily another, currently unplanned, interface type could be added.

6.1.3 Data access layer

The data access layer:

- stores and retrieves data, typically using a database management system, although flat files can also be used;
- ensures that data is stored in the correct form;
- insulates the business logic layer from knowledge of how data is stored and retrieved.

Similarly to the presentation layer, there can be a coordination, or mapping, layer in the data access layer that translates between the logical view of the data incorporated in the business logic layer and the actual physical formats in which the data is stored.

6.1.4 Layers and workflow

While the three-layer architecture has a long history, it has traditionally been used in the context of systems that have a user interface. We also need to consider how workflow can be accommodated.

Figure 6.2 illustrates some aspects of the interaction between the presentation layer and the business logic layer.

The objective of a business application is normally to support at least one business process, where a business process is any sequence of steps that is required to achieve some result of value to the business. The steps in a process could be carried out over a short period of time, or they could extend over days. A process could, of course, involve only a single step. The support provided by a business application for a business process can be implicit. In this case, the business application would provide support for the individual steps in the process, but it is the users of the application who string these together in the appropriate sequence to complete the process, making decisions along the way as to which

Figure 6.2

Presentation and
business logic layer
interactions

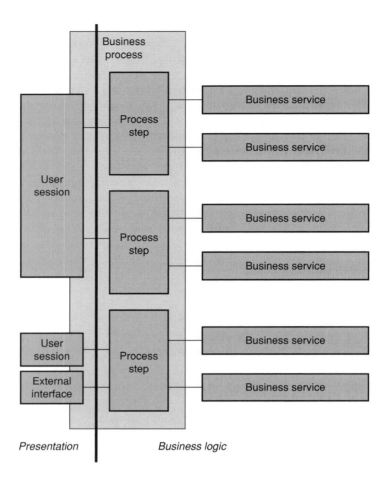

step is required next and who (or what) it should be assigned to. Alternatively, there may be explicit support for the business process, such as that provided by a workflow management system.

As an example of possible individual process steps that carry out some item of importance, let's consider the case of mortgage applications. In a simplified view, processing a mortgage application could involve the following steps.

- The mortgage broker fills in the mortgage application in collaboration with the customer.
- The lender checks the application, sends for references, and organizes a valuation of the property.
- The references are received.
- The results of the property valuation are received.
- The lender issues the mortgage offer.
- Etc.

The business application can support the first step in this process through an interactive session in which the mortgage application is filled in and submitted. It is worth noting that, for the business logic layer, the mortgage application is of no interest until it is complete. It is not interested in the user interface inter-actions that are required in order to complete the application. This is in spite of the fact that, to complete the application, the presentation layer may need to request assistance from the business logic layer to select answers to questions and to validate these answers as completion of the form progresses. It is highly desirable that the requests made of the business logic layer should be such that they are reusable in other contexts and are not simply tailored to the needs of this specific application. Otherwise, presentation changes, or a need to support a new type of external interface, will result in changes being needed to the busi-ness logic layer. This is where the external interface used has a tendency to start impacting the business logic layer.

There are two approaches to this type of requirement. In the first approach, very generic or simple methods are used allowing, for instance, individual attrib-utes to be read. In the second, the view is taken that all requests from the busi-ness logic layer should have some business meaning, such that they are not completely tied to the needs of the presentation layer. This increases the likeli-hood that the requests will be useful in other contexts where different styles of user interface are adopted.

The simple single attribute approach is completely unworkable where the presentation layer and the business logic layer may be distributed and, in my view, much better and more maintainable applications result from using requests that have a business meaning.

Some of the validation that is required may be done in the presentation layer itself, as it constructs the mortgage application. Data format checking and check-ing the presence of mandatory data and combinations of data are obvious can-didates for this, while more semantic checks will require requests to be made of the business logic layer. However, when the completed mortgage application is submitted to the business logic layer, the business logic layer must revalidate, since it can make no assumptions about the quality of the requests it receives if it is to fulfil its responsibility for ensuring data integrity.

Note that enquiry requests made by the presentation layer should be serviced by the business logic layer. Bypassing the business logic layer in order to invoke data access service requests directly would compromise the black-box character-istics of components in the business logic layer by exposing their use of data access components. This would make it impossible to simply replace a business component – instead, impact analysis and code changes to suit the internal structure of the new business component would be required.

Figure 6.2 also indicates that there is not necessarily a one-to-one relationship between a user's session and a process step. Users' sessions can terminate before a process step is complete – and often do when a dial-up connection is used! A user could also complete more than one step in a process at the same session. And more than one user or other external agent could be involved in the completion of a single process step.

While the figure shows user sessions associated only with process steps, there could also be user interaction, and therefore presentation layer logic, associated with the management of the workflow as a whole. There could be a user interface, for instance, to allow a user to decide which individuals to allocate process steps to.

Figure 6.2 also shows business services. In the context of components, we would expect these services to be grouped into components so that one component offers a number of services.

While the user interface is one route via which requests come in that must be presented to the business logic layer, requests can also come in other ways. For instance, messages may arrive from other businesses, or events may occur (time-triggered or otherwise) that should be translated into requests that are handled by the business logic layer. The role of the presentation layer is to insulate the business logic layer from the specifics of how these events occur, so that all it needs to deal with is the business impact of the event or communication.

6.1.5 Transaction boundaries

I said that responsibility for the integrity of data lies with the business logic layer. The important point for the business logic layer is that no transaction should be committed that is only partial or leaves data in an inconsistent state. This has implications for the types of request that can be made on the business logic layer. At the end of a request, it should be valid for any changes that have been made to be committed. Otherwise, the integrity of the data cannot be ensured.

But should the business logic layer actually commit the changes, or can this be left to the presentation layer (as it quite frequently is)? If you take workflow requirements into account, it seems clear that transactions should be committed within the scope of any workflow, or control, layer and I have positioned this as part of the business logic layer because it is concerned with corporate needs rather than those of the end user. In fact, no process step in a workflow should be allowed to complete if a transaction is still open. (This does not exclude the possibility that the result of a subsequent process step may involve undoing an action carried out by an earlier one.)

However, if we start building transaction commit logic into our business components, what will we do if we find we should in fact build a new component that uses services from our existing component? At this point, the idea of allowing the component execution environment to help us manage transaction boundaries becomes very attractive. A transaction within one component could then be subsumed into a larger transaction, for instance, with the component execution environment taking responsibility for deciding when the transaction is actually complete and should be committed. (See also the discussion of transaction management in Chapter 5.)

6.1.6 Distribution

Note that layers are not identical with tiers. Tiers relate to the distribution of software between separate computers in a network, whereas layers relate to the internal structure of the software. Layers do provide logical points at which to distribute software, and distribution often does follow the boundary between presentation logic, business logic, and data access logic. However, it is often necessary to soften this division by putting proxies on the remote side of a distribution divide. Proxies stand in for a component on the remote side of the communication channel. They handle logic that is best executed locally.

A possible architecture, depending on the requirements of an application, could look like that shown in Figure 6.3.

Admittedly, this figure shows a rather degenerate case, with the maximum number of proxies. Fewer proxies might be needed, or none. However, the figure's purpose is to show that layers themselves can require some level of distribution. Different components within a layer could be placed on different hosts. For an individual component that has a proxy on another platform, the main requirement is that the client should not require awareness of how the component is distributed, or of whether it is co-located or not.

6.1.7   The layered architecture and J2EE

In documentation relating to J2EE, reference can be found to the three layers that form the basis of the layered architecture described here. The documentation also refers to a number of tiers, where software is expected to be distributed between tiers that reside on separate computers in a network. Table 6.1 shows how J2EE tiers and component types map to the layered architecture, based on an interpretation of the J2EE documentation.

The split of controllers between the web tier and the EJB tier reflects the distinction between coordination logic that is required in the presentation layer and control logic that belongs in the business logic layer.

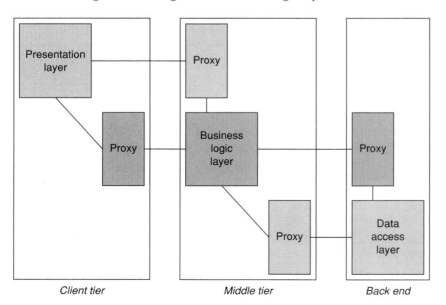

Figure 6.3
Distribution and the use of proxies

Table 6.1 Relationship between J2EE and a layered architecture

J2EE tier/ component type	Role	Subtypes	May include:		
			Presentation logic	Business logic	Data access logic
Client tier					
Web client	Connects to web tier. Executes on a desktop or other browser host usually inside a web browser of a browser plug-in. Uses HTML, applets, JavaScript, XML It is not usually transaction-capable (since it uses HTTP rather than IIOP)	Web browser Java applet Browser plug-in Standalone web client	X	X	
Application client	GUI programs on a desktop, with access to J2EE EJB tier. They are transaction-capable, implying the presence in practice of business logic	Java Visual Basic C++	X	(X)	
EIS client	Connects to an EIS resource		X	X	
Middle tier					
Web tier	Web applications using CGI, servlets, JSPs, JavaBeans Front components manage other components, handle HTTP requests, and convert them into a form that an application can understand. They provide a single point of entry into an application Presentation components are built using JSP or servlets The controllers are split between the web tier and the EJB tier. The EJB tier controller should not be web-tier specific, i.e. should be capable of responding to requests from a different client tier	Front components Presentation components Request processor Web tier controller (proxy) and EJB tier controller JavaBeans components (View data)	X		
EJB tier	Business logic components	Session beans (stateful and stateless)	X	X	
		Entity beans		X	
		Data access objects			X
Enterprise information systems (EIS)				X	X

I would expect to see the management of an item such as a shopping cart to be positioned as part of the presentation layer, although some application examples I have seen position it as if it were business logic.

6.2 Component types

Based on the layered architecture previously described, we can identify the different types of component we will use.

6.2.1 Business components

Business components will contain the logic that falls into the business logic layer. So they will contain the core business-related logic that represents what the end user would regard as the subject matter of the software. They are responsible for ensuring that business rules are observed and for maintaining the integrity of corporate business data. As discussed previously, the logic they include can be common business logic or department-specific logic.

Business components contain two types of construct:

- workflow or control logic
- business objects.

These two types of construct subdivide the business logic layer into two further layers.

Usually, control logic and business objects will be building blocks that are used internally within a component, rather than being separated into distinct components. However, it is also possible for a business component to contain only control logic or only business objects.

So what are business objects and how is control logic to be differentiated?

6.2.1.1 Business objects

A business object is any entity that participates in a business process, has a unique identity, and has a life cycle that can be expressed as a series of state changes. An example is *Customer*. Business objects have operations that they can be asked to carry out on themselves, potentially modifying their own state. They have attributes, the values of which describe their state. Their data structure may be complex – it can include structures and repeating groups of attributes. Any instance of a business object (e.g. the customer "John Smith") has its own unique identity and its own values for the attributes in its data structure, not shared values.

Modeling business objects introduces a new level of abstraction into the business model, as compared with a fully normalized model. A business object's data structure might include data from several normalized tables. By introducing a coarser-grained grouping of data, we reduce the complexity of our business model and thereby improve our ability to deal with it.

Normally, the data contained in a business object is important to the business and will be retained in the database – made persistent, in other words.

Usually, a business object will correspond to a business concept and will be something a *business user* thinks of as a single thing. For instance, a business user is likely to think of an order as a single thing, including its order items, but is unlikely to think that order items are a necessary part of a product. (The *developer* may model a business object using more than one entity in an entity-relationship model – *Orders* aggregate *OrderItems*, for example.)

This natural, common-sense grouping of data is based on our real-life perception of what an object is – something that is a coherent whole and can be separated from other coherent wholes, which we can often demonstrate by moving it from one physical environment to another. It is the internal coherence of an object and the fact that it can be separated from other objects that makes the object principle so pertinent to defining a useful software component. For these are precisely the qualities we want from a software component:

- coherence, so that we have in one place everything that is needed for a particular purpose;
- separability, so that we can use the same software component in multiple contexts, without it dragging its environment with it.

This is what makes business objects a useful building block with which to construct business components.

It is likely that the use of business objects will become the norm over a period of time, as component environments (e.g. EJBs) increasingly provide special services for business objects, particularly to manage database update. (See, for instance, the EJB specification's coverage of a query language and of bean-managed and container-managed persistence.)

6.2.1.2 Control logic

Control logic is logic that does not naturally belong in business objects. This generally means logic that relates to transactions that affect multiple objects or that relates to the management of a business process.

In its simplest form, a business component might contain control logic relating to a single logical unit of work.[1] Normally, no rollback or commit statement should be placed inside a business component. This ensures the possibility of combining logical units of work into larger transactions. Services from different business components can then be combined into larger transactions that were not necessarily envisaged when a participating business component was first developed.

---

1. A logical unit of work is a set of updates that should either succeed as a unit or fail as a unit. In other words, either all the updates involved in the logical unit of work should be committed to the database, or none of the updates involved should be made. While a transaction usually includes only one logical unit of work, in principle more than one can be combined into a single transaction.

Usually, a business component will be capable of handling more than one unit of work. It will offer more than one service, where each service allows an enquiry to be carried out or an update operation that corresponds to a logical unit of work.

6.2.1.3 Interactions between business object operations and control logic

Business object operations can be invoked from control logic or can be defined as services that are available directly through the interface of the component.

Business object operations are made available as services where there is no need for additional control logic to control a transaction. This can be the case where a transaction affects only one business object. Similarly, it can be the case where more than one business object is affected, but one business object naturally contains knowledge of the updates required in the other business objects, so that there are no maintenance benefits in removing the control logic from the business object. However, commit and rollback logic should never be put in business objects, so, if the component execution environment does not handle commit and rollback on behalf of components, separate control logic must be present to handle this.

Where a business component contains only control logic, its services may:

● invoke services in other business components that contain business objects;
● invoke data services in data access components directly to enable it to respond to an enquiry affecting multiple business objects. This should only be done where an enquiry can be satisfied simply using control logic and data access services. Under no circumstances should the business rules and business logic that belong in a business object be duplicated in control logic – instead the relevant business object operation should be invoked, so that the logic is not duplicated.

Business object operations cannot invoke control logic, since this would be a communication "up" the layers.[2]

6.2.1.4 Why separate control logic and business objects?

One reason for maintaining a clear separation is that this will simplify interoperability with component architectures, such as EJB, that separate control logic and business objects into different entities. The separation can make it possible to:

● include control logic in a module that is treated as a transient process that is only active while an operation is in process within it, while a business object stays in memory even while no operation is being carried out on it;
● allow the component execution environment to provide special services for business objects, such as assistance with queries and persistence.

2. This restriction can be relaxed where an event notification mechanism is used.

6.2.1.5 *Corporate business logic and department-specific logic*

Corporate business logic:

- can be reused across an organization or across a number of organizations;
- may be less likely to change than department-specific logic;
- will, broadly speaking, be contained in business objects in the business logic layer.

Department-specific logic:

- may be specific to a department or group of departments;
- may be more likely to change than the common business logic;
- may be contained in control logic in the business logic layer;
- may be contained in application components in the presentation layer.

This division of corporate and department-specific logic between different component types is not hard and fast. A number of alternative situations may exist.

1 Department-specific, or application-specific, requirements often relate to the presentation and manipulation of corporate data. These requirements can be handled in the presentation layer, while the business logic layer ensures corporate business rules are observed. For instance, the user interface could calculate the effect of a potential order on a customer's account balance without actually applying that update. Various alternative ways of manipulating the data, via tables, drag-and-drop, etc., can be accommodated provided they do not contravene business rules.

2 There may be business objects that are specific to a particular department. In this case, parts of all three layers (the presentation layer, the business logic layer, and the data access layer) will be department-specific.

3 There may be department-specific business rules for business objects that are used by more than one department. In this case, there will be both a department-specific and a corporate aspect to the business objects in the business logic layer, which must be carefully managed. It may be appropriate to separate these aspects into different components, using role-based techniques. (These are discussed in Section 6.4 on page 88.)

6.2.2 Application components

Application components include logic from the presentation layer. They manage the user interface (and other interfaces handled by the presentation layer) and interact with business components to provide an application that meets users' requirements.

While business components have *corporate* needs as their primary focus, application components have the *end user's* need for an integrated application as their primary focus. An application meets an identifiable set of user needs and has a scope such that the user views the application conceptually as a unified whole. An *integrated* application achieves this so that the user is not disturbed by differences between the parts, e.g. divergent user interfaces, the need to duplicate data between systems, etc.

Application component logic is less reusable than business component logic because it is specific to the user interface and to workflow, and likely to be tailored to the requirements of a particular set of users. This means it is often less obvious that there is value in dividing the application logic into application components.

There are several types of application component.

- Large-scale application components. This includes application components up to the size of an application. A large-scale application component can include a set of functions that is made available to users via the user interface, and maybe also, or instead of, batch functionality or interfaces with external systems.

- User task components. A user task component includes a single user task, or external interface task, as a whole. A single user task is an item of work that is carried out by a single user and often could be included in a longer business process or workflow as an individual process step. The use of user task components does not necessarily imply that workflow management is used (e.g. automatic allocation of tasks to users, etc.), although workflow management is not possible without user task components.

- Batch components. A batch component includes the required functionality for an individual batch job or job step.

- Subtask component. An application component may sometimes be defined for an application part, maybe looking up addresses in a postcode database, that is required in more than one user task.

6.2.3   Data access components

Data access components include:

- the mapping between the view of data that is incorporated in the business logic layer and the actual format in which it is stored;
- the physical data access to the data, handled in a way that is specific to the database or flat file system in use.

Data access components generally have a very standard format with a high potential for generation of code. The set of standard services to be included (to cover insert, update, delete, and standard types of read) can be defined as part of an organization's development standards. Additional services for non-standard enquiries normally have to be designed additionally, as required.

Often, there will be a single data access component for each business component, although a data access component may be defined for a business object.

(The scoping of data access components is discussed further in Section 6.4 on page 88.)

6.2.4 Utility components

Could there be a role for utility components that contain common logic that is reusable by all three layers and therefore does not belong to any of them? Well, yes, it is possible. But often candidate utility components will turn out to be best offered as part of the software infrastructure – logging, for instance. These services may well also be found to be platform-specific.

6.3   Wrappers and adapters

This section explains what wrappers and adapters are and how they can be used with components.

6.3.1 Wrappers

A wrapper, with what it wraps, should form an application, business, or data access component that forms part of a planned component blueprint. The resulting components have a shape and scope which is planned so that the benefits we seek from CBD will be achieved. That is to say they are not just any shape, as determined by the shape of what they wrap. Instead, their shape should be one that fits in with the overall architecture toward which we are moving. Figure 6.4 shows how wrappers are related to components.

Wrappers are "special" in that part of the functionality of the resulting component is provided by the wrapper and part is provided by what is wrapped. Wrappers can be used to:

- wrap non-componentized legacy code;
- wrap an existing component, the functionality of which requires extension;
- provide a part of a component's functionality on a different platform, e.g. on the client platform. In this case, the wrapper acts as a proxy.

Over time, or with changing circumstances, a wrapper and what it wraps could be merged without impacting the component's clients.

Any client of the component always views the combination of a wrapper and what it wraps as a single component. No client of the component should be aware that it includes a wrapper. The wrapper acts as a façade that shields the outside world from knowing how the component is structured internally.

Note that when a wrapper is used to wrap legacy code, the boundary with the legacy code can be anywhere – not just on a layer boundary. The wrapper itself is inevitably exposed to the legacy code, but no other component is since the component's services are accessed through the wrapper. Over time, the legacy part of the component may become smaller, until it is completely replaced. (See

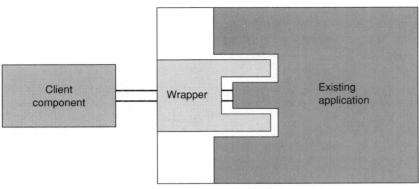

Figure 6.4
Role of a wrapper

Virtual component

Chapter 12 for details of using wrappers to extend a component's functionality, and the section on Application Integration on page 163 for one example of why a proxy may be needed to wrap part of a component's functionality on a different platform.)

6.3.2 Adapters

An adapter, unlike a wrapper, does not contain presentation, business, or data access logic itself. It merely sits between two components in order to convert between their different technical perceptions of interfaces. It is a thin piece of software that maps between the service invocation issued by a client and the service invocation expected by the used component. Similarly, it translates back from the response produced by the used component to the response expected by the client.

Figure 6.5 shows the relationship between an adapter and the components it adapts.

The role of an adapter is to insulate both client and used component from the knowledge of any incompatibilities between them. Adapter components can be required between any two components, whether these are application components, business components, or data access components. Adapters sit between components that have the shape we want, as defined by our component blueprint, but that are perhaps implemented using different technologies.

Note that adapter components should not be used to extend the functionality of the used component. This is achieved by adding a wrapper to create a new component, such as a business component or an application component. Where an adapter is used, if one of the two components is reimplemented in the same technology as the other (to use the same data formats, etc.) it should be possible simply to remove the adapter component without there being any functional loss.

Adapter components may contain:

● interface conversion – it may be necessary to convert field formats, add or discard parameters, and present parameters in a different sequence;

Figure 6.5
Adapters and
components

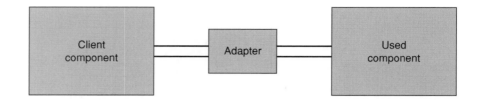

- non-standard settings – where the used component is not well encapsulated or is badly designed, it may be necessary to set switches, e.g. to indicate the database to be used;

- validation and error handling – the adapter may need to ensure that data that is passed to the used component will be acceptable. That is, the data must observe any preconditions set by the used component. The adapter must also handle all possible responses from the used component, including any error handling that is needed but is handled in a way that is not compatible with the expectations of the client component, for instance because it is technology-specific;

- security – a legacy application may use different security mechanisms from newer components. In this case the adapter component must ensure that the legacy application's security requirements are respected.

In addition, there may be conversion requirements that arise because the client component and the component whose services it uses are in different environments. It is desirable to isolate these conversion requirements, as far as possible, by using a separate technical adapter. Thus an adapter may itself split into two layers. The technical adapter should handle:

- protocol conversion, for instance connecting COM to CORBA;

- environment-related requirements, e.g. start-up of a runtime environment.

For some environments, there are software development tools that can automate the production of technical adapters to handle protocol conversion.

Does an adapter belong with the client component or the component whose services it accesses? Strictly, it belongs with neither. It is specific to the connection of a particular pair of components, and if either of the components is replaced, the adapter would no longer be useful. From the perspective of each component, the adapter belongs to the other side of the link. From an architectural perspective, it may be the case that one of the two components represents the interface in the preferred way, in which case the adapter can be regarded as being more closely connected with the other component.

6.4   Defining the scope of components

Determining the appropriate scope and contents of a component is not easy. This section discusses some of the issues for each type of component and provides some guidance. It covers types of component in the following sequence:

- business components, including coverage of business objects and control logic;
- application components;
- data access components.

6.4.1 Business components

As already discussed, business components contain two types of construct:

- business objects;
- control logic that does not belong in business objects.

6.4.1.1 Allocating business objects to components

Here are some guidelines relating to the use of business objects for CBD.

Is a business object a component?
It would be possible to define every business component so that it includes one and only one business object. However, many business objects are too small and too closely interconnected with other objects to provide useful components. Because they are interconnected, they cannot usefully be used without the business objects with which they are connected.

For this reason, it is my view that business objects should not automatically be used to provide the scope for business components. Instead, it will usually be appropriate to include one or more business objects in a business component.[3]

Using larger components that include business objects that are closely interconnected makes reuse simpler. It also makes it possible to distinguish between those components that are the real building blocks that can be used independently and those business objects that are only ever used in a predefined combination with other business objects.

There will, of course, be cases where a business component does indeed consist of a single business object. In fact, there are some business objects, such as *Party* (sometimes alternatively called *Business Partner*) that are extremely complex and have multiple aspects that are not all relevant for a single application. Such business objects are often best split between components, with one business component handling the basic core of the object, and other components handling specific roles that the object may play, for instance *Prospect* or *Customer*. Section 6.4.1.2 discusses this in greater detail.

---

3. Note that some business components will not include business objects at all, but just control logic.

Should a business object be handled by only one component, or could the same business object appear in multiple components?

From the point of view of data management, it is a valuable simplification if all processing related to one business object is contained in only one component. From a logical point of view, if a business object appears in more than one component it suggests redundancy. A good business component model will result in functionality appearing only once, therefore in only one component.

It is possible that different applications will have very different views of the same business object. This can be handled in more than one way.

- It may be that there is no business reason why the objects in question should be recognized as being the same business object. For instance, one application may require records of users for access control purposes, while another requires records of customers. A user could also be a customer, but there is no obvious business benefit in knowing details of a customer's user access rights. In such cases, two separate business objects should be identified.

- The part that is in common can be separated into one business object, with additional "role" business objects being used for the parts that are specific to a particular usage of the object. (See Section 6.4.1.2.)

Where legacy code is used (as, of course, it often will be), there may be no choice other than to have two components that handle the same business object. An organization's CBD strategy should include a migration strategy toward an architecture in which the business object is handled by only one component. In the meantime, ensuring consistency of behavior from both components may be difficult.

Example problem case: addresses

There are arguments that suggest different possible directions for addresses.

1 More than one customer may live at the same address, but this is not usually significant from a business point of view. This suggests that an address should be treated as part of the same component as the customer.

2 Zipcode management applications make an obvious component that can be used by all components that include an address. It seems logical to put all address management capabilities in a single component.

3 While a Zipcode management application may be used for national addresses, foreign addresses are likely to require different handling.

A best solution to these different forces will often be to treat each address as a dependent part of its owner (e.g. customer) not seeking to store any given address only once, while using an address management component for all address-related operations.

6.4.1.2 Role objects

Different groups of people in different business units often have different perspectives on the same objects. When developing an application, requirements could be identified for the application to deal with customers, suppliers, and agents. However, when corporate data modelers are confronted with this, they are likely to tell us that we should be using a *Person*, or even more abstractly, a *Party* business object. *Party* represents the business concept that all the different usages have in common and it also includes the common attributes and operations, for instance catering for contact information. But how can we reconcile this with the fact that *Party* has the specific role of *Customer* in our specific application, and that the user interface must certainly present *Customers* rather than *Parties*?

Roles offer a way of approaching this issue. We can use a common corporate-level business object *Party* that deals with the common attributes and processing requirements for *Parties* in all the places where that business concept is needed. We can then deal with the application-specific requirements using another component that adds a particular role to *Party*. See Figure 6.6 for an example.

The role object (e.g. *Customer*) shares its identity with the *Party* object. It has the same primary key and is related to a single *Party* object.[4] The role object extends the *Party* object with additional attributes and operations. It may have relationships of its own.

The role object is able to incorporate the attributes and operations of the *Party* object. It can service requests that could otherwise be directed at the *Party* object, either by simply passing on these requests or by adding logic that is specific to the role object and to the role that is played by the *Party* object in the specific context.

This raises the question, "Should the application direct requests to the role object or to the *Party* object?" The answer depends on what the application is dealing with. If it is concerned with the *Party* as a *Customer*, all its requests should be directed to the *Customer* object. If it is dealing with all *Parties*, regardless of their role, the request should be directed to the *Party* object. And, of course, the objects must be designed so that this will work, so that functionality contained in *Party* is genuinely context-independent.

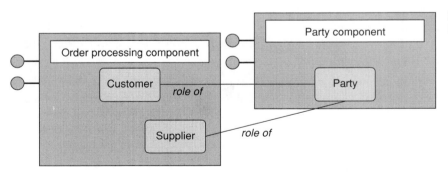

Figure 6.6
Use of roles

---

4. Less commonly, a *Party* object could be associated with more than one role object of a given type if there is some other context associated with the role that distinguishes each of the roles. Also, in complicated cases, roles can themselves have roles.

6.4.1.3   Control logic

A business component can contain control logic relating to a single logical unit of work, or to more than one unit of work. Here are some guidelines with respect to incorporating control logic into business components.

What set of services should I combine into one business component?
The basic principle governing the allocation of transactions to a single business component is the expectation that, where one of these transactions is required by an application, the other transactions are also likely to be required.

Generally, it is useful to group together, in one business component, transactions that are related because they belong to the same *business process*. A business process usually involves a sequence of events that occurs over a period of time and thus can involve multiple database updates. These different, associated database updates, that affect the same set of business objects, can be usefully grouped together into a single business component.

You might think of combining transactions from different business processes into a business component, but this isn't likely to pass the test that transactions should be combined into one business component if they are likely to be required together.

For long-running business processes, it may be unlikely that a single application will deal with the whole business process. In this case, parts of the business process should be separated into different business components. It is desirable to try to define the scope of the component such that it is small enough to be usable by a single application without offering many unused services, but large enough to group together transactions that are related. There is, of course, no requirement that every service offered should be used by every client.

6.4.1.4   Defining the scope of business components

The simplest type of business component to identify is one that contains control logic for transactions that are part of a single business process and, additionally, the business objects these transactions affect. This provides a default scope for a business component.

The following considerations will help define the scope of other types of business component.

- Group business objects together in one business component where there are strong relationships between the objects, e.g. mandatory relationships and/or where business processes affect a set of related objects (these two criteria tend to occur together).
- Where multiple business processes affect a common set of business objects, it is useful to define both:
  - a business component that contains these reused business objects;
  - for each business process, a separate business component that contains control logic only, plus any business objects that are specific to the business process.

- For key business objects, such as *Party*, that tend to be required for many business processes but with different data and processing requirements in each, separate out the common core of the object into one component and put role objects in other components to handle role-specific aspects.

- Where a business component needs to manage a relationship between two business objects, either:
  - include both business objects in the business component;
  - include one business object in a business component that is a client of the business component that contains the other business object;
  - make the business component use two business components, each of which contains one of the managed business objects.[5]

- Do not put together objects that are not involved in the same business processes and are not associated with each other.

Further guidelines for constructing business components

Consider variation points. For instance, accounts may be similar but use different accrual algorithms. Warehouses may use different algorithms for determining where to store containers. It may be possible to isolate variation points into components, allowing each variation to be handled by substituting a different component. It may be useful to define a component to handle complex calculations – for instance, a quotation engine, an accruals calculation engine, etc.

Bundle functionality that can be used by more than one business unit (department or location). For instance:

- financial salesperson competency – a salesperson retains competency by selling the products for which the salesperson has passed exams. His or her competency is updated by the human resources or training departments as exams are passed, and by the sales department as products are sold. It is desirable to define this functionality only once, not to define it once for each user of the functionality.

Do not bundle together facilities that are required in multiple contexts with facilities that are required only in a specific context. For instance:

- maintain financial salesperson competency – because this service is used in multiple contexts, it would not be useful to bundle it with human resources requirements such as "maintain address", or sales requirements such as "calculate achievement of targets". This would prevent it from being reused.

It is worth noting that focussing on business processes and business objects, rather than on the set of miscellaneous requirements of a particular organizational unit or location, will make it natural to define appropriate, reusable business components rather than ones that thwart reuse by the inappropriate bundling of services.

---

5. Tactics for managing relationships are discussed in more detail in Chapter 12.

Should business components be packaged to include data access components?

Business components may be packaged to include or exclude data access, but should always be architected such that, if data access is included, it can readily be removed or replaced. Often, data access will be packaged with the business component because it will often be the case that, wherever the component is used, data is always stored in the same database.

There are reasons for packaging and deploying data access separately when:

- the component may be used by different departments within the organization that store data in different databases;
- the component is to be sold to different organizations, each with different data storage requirements.

6.4.2 Application components

When considering the scope of application components, we need to consider both:

- how to scope the application as a whole; and
- how to subdivide the application into application components.

6.4.2.1 The scope of applications

The end objective is to define applications which meet end users' needs by grouping functionality in a way that allows them to carry out their activities in a coordinated manner. Often, application definition is an intuitive process based on the users' own perceptions of their needs, and is not a taxing task.

For large-scale applications, there are many guidelines as to how to partition systems into separate projects and subsystems. These guidelines are still relevant when considering the appropriate scope of an application. They are based on identifying:

- the business processes and workflows to be supported by the application(s);
- the business objects affected by the workflows;
- the organizational units responsible for (parts of) the workflows;
- the locations at which (parts of) the workflows are carried out;
- a view as to the cohesiveness or separateness of different parts of the application.

Useful considerations include:

- the organization – it is desirable that tasks carried out by the same group of people should be in the same application;
- the location of data – is some data used primarily by people at one location? If so, then this data and processing can be placed in a separate application;
- variations in usage and perspective – usually different departments within an

organization have varying perspectives. It is worth considering whether to define an application to meet the specific perspective of a specific group of people, or whether a standardized application can meet the needs of multiple groups. Obviously, a standardized application will have lower costs, and will often be the right solution, even when users resist it because they are convinced their needs are special. However, the lower costs must be balanced against the extent to which a single application can meet different departments' specific requirements. By combining common business components with some department-specific application or maybe business components, it may be possible to meet departmental requirements better.

It is also worth considering (still bearing in mind that the objective is to meet user needs):

- business processes and workflows – it may be useful to put a workflow as a whole in the same application;
- data usage and data update – it may be useful to consider grouping into an application processes which update the same business object.

6.4.2.2   The scope of application components

Application logic is less reusable than business components because it is specific to the user interface and is likely to be tailored to the requirements of a particular set of users.[6] This means that it is often less obvious that there is value in dividing the application logic into application components.

There are several relevant levels of definition for application components. It may be worth defining large-granularity application components that correspond to subapplications, handling a subset of the functionality of the application. This can enable individual application components to be developed by different project teams. Where a subset of an application (e.g. a branch of a menu hierarchy) can be reused in multiple applications, this should be defined as an application component.

Note, however, that similarities in the requirements of different sets of users may be accidental. Two groups of users with different management may have different priorities and change requests. This means that if two organizational units start by using the same application components, it may be necessary to allow their usage to diverge.

It can be useful to have application components that correspond to business components and are capable of managing standard access to the business objects included in the business component. These application components can then be incorporated into multiple applications.

---

6. The user interface *style* can be standardized, leading to opportunities for the use of frameworks and for code generation that can be incorporated in the software infrastructure.

Within an application component, it is frequently useful to adopt the approach of defining *user task* components, where each user task component includes a single user task as a whole. A user task component can also be created to handle an external interface. Division into user task components is essential where workflow is used. Even where it isn't, it helps produce a well-modularized application that is likely to be more flexible and maintainable as a result. It eases the development process (by divide and conquer). The user task components also offer a good type of component for potential reuse in other applications.

Similarly, it is normally useful to define batch components for each batch job or job step, since each job step will normally be implemented as a separate executable anyway. It is sometimes useful to define a subtask component for application code that is shared between multiple user tasks.

Usually, it will not be useful to define components at a finer level of granularity than a user task or batch component, with occasional exceptions for subtask components. Consider the possibility of defining a component for a reusable window, for instance. The overhead of defining this as a separately executable component is not usually justified. Generally, it will be more useful to reuse such items at construction time rather than to build separate executable components.

6.4.3   Data access components

Usually, it will be useful to define a data access object for each business object, and maybe an additional data access object, or objects, to handle queries that join data from different data access objects. But, just as business objects should not necessarily all become components, nor should their corresponding data access objects.

Usually, it will be appropriate to define a single data access component per business component. This component can be packaged with the business component or it can be kept separate so that it can be replaced for use with different databases.

In some environments, data access layers may be completely generated and therefore not require separate definition.

6.5   Component specification

This section gives a view of what should be included in the definition of a component.

6.5.1   Basics of the component interface

A component offers (provides) one or more *services* for use by other components or non-componentized software. (A component *is* allowed to use its own services.) A service is a function or procedure that can be invoked by specifying the service name and providing input arguments. On completion, the service returns output values.

For the sake of clarity, I am making a distinction between *services*, which provide the public interface to a component, and *operations*, which are similar to services but available for use only within the component. Business objects, for instance, will offer operations for invocation within the component.

Services are grouped into *interfaces*. Each interface groups a set of related services that share some common purpose, so that typically a user of one service is likely to require the use of other services in the interface. As an example, an interface might include the set of services used to open, read, write, and close a file or communications link. The lollipop shown on the side of components in Figure 6.6 represents an interface. This diagramatic convention is based on conventions used with Microsoft's COM.

All the services that a component offers are potentially available for use by any client. A component should not choose its clients, since this would build into it undue knowledge of its context. Clients are free to use a subset of the interfaces provided by a component, and may choose to use only selected services within an interface.

The above model is sufficiently generic to cover the types of component model currently available, but existing component models do vary. An EJB session bean offers only one interface, apart from its home interface. By way of contrast, COM and CCM components can offer multiple interfaces.

6.5.2 Client components and component assemblies

Components that invoke services in other components effectively require the presence of those components, or at least of a component that provides the interface(s) they use.

This can be resolved in two ways.

1 *Including a component.* The component can be delivered as part of a component assembly that *includes* components whose interfaces it uses. In this case, the process of building a configuration is simplified as there are fewer dependencies to resolve.

2 *Using a component.* The component specification can state the interfaces the component requires. When a configuration is built, the software developer creating the configuration has to ensure components are present that meet these requirements.

6.5.3 Component specification

There are two parts to a component specification – the part that is required by the component model used (which varies depending on the component model used), and the additional textual information that should be provided for use by component assemblers. The following are useful parts of a specification, including both types of information:

- name and brief description;
- provided interfaces – these are the interfaces that the component offers for use by its clients. The services included in the interface are listed. Where there is more than one interface, each interface should be named, its purpose briefly described, and the services included in it listed;
- required interfaces – interfaces the component uses should be specified. It is not necessary to allocate the interfaces to a specific component;
- events published and events consumed – these types of interface allow a component to publish events asynchronously that other components may consume, or to consume events that other components publish;
- component characteristics – this includes information required by the component execution environment, such as:
  - ability to locate instances of the component using a primary key;
  - whether the component is stateless, has conversational state, or is persistent;
  - transactional support: does the component manage transactions or leave this to the component execution environment? If the latter, can it join an existing transaction or does it require a new one?
- additional information as relevant – quality assurance status, test pack, guarantees (e.g. service levels), caveats/limitations, support contacts, component size, environment considerations (e.g. operating system and platform). Within an organization, the technical architecture should include standard technical information on technologies and platforms for different types of component so it should only be necessary to note information that is not standard or varies between components.

6.5.4 Defining services

A black-box specification of each service should be provided for use by application assemblers. This could include:

- service type (enquiry or update);
- preconditions;
- input and output parameters, including a specification of ranges of values for the parameters, and information as to which input parameters are optional or mandatory;
- any error conditions (business logic-related or technical);[7]
- description of the purpose of the service, including any updates carried out.

---

7. Development standards should specify standard error types.

Putting component-based development into practice

Suppose you believe that adopting a component-based approach could bring benefits within your organization. What do you need to do in order to move toward this type of development approach?

This chapter builds on the previous three chapters and outlines a set of steps that can be used to create an initial CBD strategy and to refine this strategy over time. In broad overview, the steps are as follows.

- First, clarify what you are trying to achieve. What benefits are you looking for? Also, what do you expect the scope of the use of a component-based approach to be?
- Review the business domain and systems for which you plan to use components, so that you can map out, at a high level, how you think they would ideally be covered by components.
- Review your existing systems to see how they map to the ideal vision.
- Define the technological framework you will use for components, covering the software architecture and infrastructure issues that were outlined in Chapter 5.
- Define the organizational approach that you will take, both with respect to the business-related issues discussed in Chapter 4 and with respect to the organization of the people involved in the development initiative itself.
- Finally, modify your approach to program planning so that over time your component strategy will come into effect.

These steps make it apparent that the main requirement for moving to a component-based approach is simply to adopt a planned approach to software development, colored of course by an understanding of CBD. We have to plan anyway, however informally we do it. For a component-based strategy, we can simply approach the task with a modified mindset.

The remainder of this chapter describes in more detail how each of the above tasks can be carried out.

7.1   Defining the scope and expected benefits of a component-based development initiative

It is worth starting by considering and documenting:

- what benefits are sought from adoption of a component-based approach;
- whether components are relevant to your organization;
- what part of the organization they are relevant to and what should be the scope of the initiative to introduce the use of components.

7.1.1   Key drivers for adopting a component-based approach

You need a good reason before engaging in any change in development practice and it was the objective of the first part of this book to explain some of the reasons why a move to a component-based approach can bring benefits. However, it is desirable to consider what benefits *you* expect to get from a component-based approach, and it is also worth reviewing progress over a period of time to determine whether these benefits are being delivered, and if they aren't, why not.

Some of the possible reasons for moving toward a component-based approach are listed briefly below.

- Moving to components will result in a better architected application portfolio that:
  - has fewer duplications of functionality, improving consistency and maintainability and reducing maintenance costs;
  - makes it easier to integrate legacy applications with new applications and to migrate from legacy applications over a period of time;
  - is easier to adapt in the face of reorganizations of the business and changes in the way business is done;
  - makes it easier to manage the differing requirements of departments, while still handling corporate-wide requirements in a consistent way across the organization as a whole;
  - makes it possible to develop new software more quickly, as existing components can be leveraged;
  - improves the quality and maintainability of the software through the use of an architected approach.
- Adoption of a component-based approach fits well with the use of current development technologies, such as J2EE and .NET.

- Adoption of a component-based approach fits well with the trend toward the development of Web services, available over the Internet.
- Adoption of a component-based approach will improve the saleability of software products, or enable an organization to purchase packaged software that can be tailored more readily to the organization's specific needs.
- Adoption of a component-based approach will allow a software house (or software product vendor) to create components for a software product line, enabling the flexible production of solutions that meet different customer requirements.

7.1.2   Counter-indicators

It may be hard to introduce an architected approach into an organization that has no record of controlled software development, or into one with a poor record of successful project completion (due, for instance, to frequent changes in direction). In these cases, it is likely to be best to start with modest targets and a limited scope.

Other cases in which a component-based approach is unlikely to be relevant are where existing software largely meets requirements and the rate of change is slow, or where the organization is fully committed to the use of packaged software and does not need purpose-built software or software that is tailored to its specific needs.

7.1.3   Scope of a component adoption initiative

As discussed in Chapter 4, the scope of a component adoption initiative must depend on the scope of influence of the sponsors of the initiative and on their focus of interest. The wider the scope, the more the potential benefits – and the greater the risk of failure. It is not realistic to include areas of the business that are outside the sponsors' scope of control. It is also not a good idea to attempt a scope that will stretch beyond the bounds of the knowledge of key staff, or that will be too large for them to keep a conceptual grip on.

It is also worth considering which parts of the business have most need of an improved process. These may be areas where the IT department finds it difficult to keep up with the speed of change:

- where an Internet presence is required and the speedy adaptation of existing applications to new requirements is key;
- where mergers and acquisitions mean adopting parts of different organizations' systems, rather than standardizing on one selected set of existing systems (a more desirable choice where it is possible);
- where there is a high frequency of organizational change to which systems must adapt;
- where there is a high level of change in the business, for instance where new products must be introduced quickly.

The use of components is also particularly relevant where there is a lot of duplication between systems.

7.2 Defining a component blueprint

A component blueprint defines the planned components for the business, using the types defined in the component model. The considerations involved in selecting a set of component types were discussed in Chapter 6.

The component blueprint provides an overall map for the organization that covers, at a high level, its business processes and business object model. The model shows how the business-related software can be broken down into components, making it possible to devise a strategy for achieving this over time. It provides a "target" architecture, toward which the application portfolio can gradually migrate.

A component blueprint will usually give business components the lion's share of the attention, with application components generally being considered during the course of standard program planning as individual applications are planned and developed.

Obviously, an invitation to model an organization's business could result in a lengthy exercise with results of little or no value, and this must be avoided. The ideal people to produce a component blueprint are those who already have responsibility for the functionality provided for different business areas. If these people don't exist it may be appropriate to reconsider your organization and to look at how you can introduce and develop such functional experts.

The inputs required in order to produce a component blueprint are:

- an organization chart, with a mapping to locations;
- a list of business processes;
- a business object model.

Producing an organization chart hardly requires further explanation, so I will discuss further only the last two of these inputs.

7.2.1 Identifying business processes

Business processes are usually triggered by a business event. They have a business goal that can usefully be stated briefly. The steps involved in a business process can be listed and the organizational units and locations at which these steps are carried out identified.

Table 7.1 shows an example of a business process and the steps involved in it.

Table 7.1 Example of a business process

Sell investment product:
– Advise on suitable products
– Process received application
– Underwrite policy
– Issue policy
– Initiate premium collection

Note that detailed business process analysis is not necessary when defining a component blueprint.

7.2.2 Building a business object model

Building a business object model for the area of the business which is within the scope of a CBD initiative has some resemblance to the practice of defining a corporate data model. However, the granularity of the model is coarser – business objects rather than relational tables – and it is not necessary to go into the full details of defining all the attributes of each object.

It is not the objective to capture the complexity of the real world – a failing sometimes encountered in corporate data models – but simply to produce a model from which applications can be built that meet user requirements. This is a planning level model in which unnecessary complexity would simply be a distraction. Detailed modeling is the task of individual development projects.

You can identify business objects by considering the objects required in the business to support the identified business processes. Analysts who are expert in the area can do this simply by consulting their own knowledge of the business domain, but it is likely to be useful to draw on existing data models and system documentation, and on the knowledge of business experts.

For each business object, it is useful to record:

- the business object name – this should be as self-explanatory as possible. Ideally the name should be understandable by the layman;

- a brief description – a description of one or two lines that explains the nature of the objects. It can sometimes be useful to define an object type by exclusion – by saying what is not included;

- the relationships between objects – these should be named so that the meaning of the relationship is recorded. The cardinality of the relationship should also be specified;

- the attributes – generally, it is not necessary to record attributes, but they can be recorded if this provides a good way of understanding the nature of the object. If attributes are recorded, a brief description of each is likely to be necessary so that its meaning can be remembered later.

The business objects identified should represent things and concepts at the level of abstraction at which the business user deals with them. For instance, even if two financial instruments are to all intents and purposes the same in terms of their processing needs, if the business user sees them as two separate business objects then that is how they should be modeled. A supertype can be included in the model to capture the commonality.

It is true that, when it comes to components, the abstract concept, and thus the supertype, is of particular interest. But in the business object model, it is important to capture the concrete things the business user recognizes, so that these can be correlated with the software that is produced.

It is not necessary to break up business objects into smaller parts. For instance, you do not need to model an order as consisting of an order header and order lines. It is only relevant to model the composition of a business object where the detail that would otherwise be omitted is key to understanding the business at the level at which the business user deals with it.

It is not necessary to resolve many-to-many relationships unless the link entity is itself recognizably a business object with significant behavior associated with it.

Figure 7.1 shows an example of business objects for the business process shown in Table 7.1.

7.2.3 Developing a component blueprint

The purpose of the component blueprint is to provide a big picture or vision of how the business domains that are in scope can be componentized, focussing on business components. It presents an ideal set of components, toward which the organization can aim to move over the course of time. This set of components should not be biassed toward the shape of existing systems, which will be taken into account when defining the development program itself, as part of program planning.

How best to define the scope of business components was discussed in Chapter 6. This is done by reviewing the business processes and the business objects involved in those processes, and by considering the parts of the organization involved in the steps of the business process, and the locations at which business process steps are carried out.

Figure 7.1
Business objects for
"Sell investment
product"

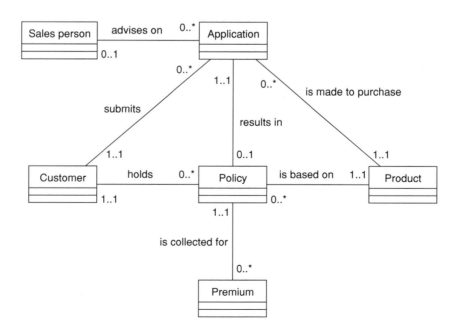

For each business component identified, it is useful to record:

- the business processes or business process steps that the component handles;
- the business objects that the component includes (if any);
- the services that the component offers, in high-level terms. (It is not necessary to identify every service the component will offer.)

Dependencies between components should be identified. Which components will require the services of which other components? Circular dependencies should be avoided if possible.

A summary-level component diagram can be used to show the business components that have been identified and the dependencies between them. Where a component could be used without another component in some contexts, it is desirable to avoid a dependency on that component. For instance, the existence of *Orders* presupposes the existence of *Products*, so an *Order* component can reasonably use the services of a *Product* component. *Products*, however, should be able to exist without *Orders*, and may need to if the *Product* component is reused in another context, so it is desirable that the *Product* component should not use the services of an *Order* component.

Where there are relationships between business objects in different business components, one business component must manage the relationship. Diagrams can be used to show relationships between business objects in different business components. The diagram can show:

- the business objects that are included in the managing component;
- the components that provide services used by the managing component (and so are required by it). These will include the other component or components involved in a managed relationship;
- the related business object in the other component(s) and the relationship that spans the components.

It is not necessary to show all the business objects included in the components.

For examples of this type of diagram, see Section 12.5 on page 157. UML[1] notation is also usable for diagraming component blueprints, although it is not specifically designed for it.

It is difficult to list a set of points to consider when producing a model that will optimize the level of commonality and reusability across the business domain because these depend on a detailed understanding of the business domain and also on our gradually evolving perception of opportunities. For instance, at a particular point in time many businesses perceive a need for unified customer management, but there is no guideline that could lead you to mechanically identify the need for this.

Some aspects need consideration.

- Potential for identifying a basic abstraction of which different variants are used. For instance, can all investment products be built from a set of standard

---

1. The Unified Modeling Language (UML) is an OO modeling language that has been standardized by the OMG. For its specification, see www.omg.org

components and handled in a similar way? Can a standard set of components be defined for insurance product definition? Not all such ideas are worth pursuing – there may be too many variations for a common model to be viable.

● Whether business processes are identical except in their mode of presentation. For instance, sale of a product (insurance, etc.) is basically the same whether it is delivered by a door-to-door salesman, over the phone, in a store, or by letter. The differences can often be handled by application components, while the business component remains the same. Similarly, container movements in a warehouse should be fundamentally the same whether the movement is automated, radio-controled, or manual.

● What is intrinsic to the nature of a problem and what is specific about the way a company is dealing with it. If the model can separate the two, changes are likely to have less impact. The specific aspects (e.g. the actual physical layout of a warehouse) can be modeled such that they can be modified by changing database definitions rather than code. Here, there is a trade-off between flexibility, the speed of development, and maybe the performance of the end system. A more flexible solution that involves more development effort and results in poorer performance may not be justifiable if the organization's practices are unlikely to change.

7.2.3.1 Affinity analysis

Affinity analysis can be used to determine with which business processes or process steps business objects are most closely associated. The analysis closely associates a business object and the process that creates it, followed by a lower affinity rating for update, followed by delete, then read.

The example shown in Table 7.2 takes the previously analyzed business process "Sell investment product" and maps a more detailed view of the process steps to the business objects. Customer-related information is needed for this process, as well as for many other business processes. This makes it an obvious candidate as a business component.

The *Letter* object – certainly requiring further analysis down the line, but I am trying not to be pedantic at this stage – suggests there could be some value in a document manager component that is concerned with the common aspects of outbound documents or communications. It could be useful for the business logic layer to produce business communications in a format that does not presuppose a particular medium for the communication (e.g. letter, e-mail, etc.). There can be business reasons for preferring one communication medium over another for a particular type of communication, which would be logic to be included in business components. However, it can be left to an application component in the presentation layer to actually format the communication to fit the chosen medium and to dispatch it.

For this example, there might be three business components.

1 Customer information manager:

　　– a business-wide component;

Table 7.2   Business object to business process matrix

	Customer	Product	Policy	Application	Sales person	Premium	Letter
Respond to inbound contact	R				R		C
Make outbound contact	R				R		C
Capture customer information	CRU				R		
Provide financial advice	RU	R			R		
Identify solutions to needs		R					
Provide performance illustrations	R	R					C
Handle application	R	R		C	R		C
Underwrite policy		R		RU			RU
Issue policy	R	R	C	UD			C
Initiate premium collection	R					C	CU

C – create
R – read
U – update
D – delete

  – provides identification information about any person, or external organization, that has received advice about any product, has applied for any product, or has purchased any product.

2 Document registry:

  – a general-purpose component;

  – creates, distributes, and tracks any document that supports a savings and investment product, including periodic statements, and cancellation and surrender documents;

  – excludes any outbound marketing communication documents.

3 Policy underwriter:

  – a highly specific, data-driven logic engine;

  – applies underwriting rules to any application for a savings, investment, or protection product.

7.3   Auditing current systems

In addition to reviewing the business domain and systems for which we plan to use components, and mapping out a component blueprint, it is necessary to understand our existing systems so that we can see how well they map to the ideal vision. The vision and the reality are then tools that can be used when determining how to handle requirements for change in a way that improves the level of componentization of the application portfolio.

An inventory of existing systems and a view of their overall status at a high level is really a prerequisite for any form of program planning. More detailed investigation of existing systems does not need to be done upfront, but will need to be carried out as part of feasibility studies to determine how new requirements will be met.

The following activities are relevant to an audit of current systems:

1   Creating an inventory of current systems.

2   Producing a hot list of systems for which componentization is particularly relevant.

These activities are discussed in more detail below.

7.3.1   Creating an inventory of current systems

The purpose of this task is to identify the systems within the scope of the componentization initiative, and to establish key facts about them in terms of data, function, and platform. It is desirable to determine the key facts from existing catalogs or knowledgeable staff, rather than through time-consuming searches through code, etc.

The list of systems in use by the business, within the scope of the initiative, should include:

- purpose-built applications;
- software packages addressing business functionality, e.g. payroll and general ledger;
- systems in use within IT itself, e.g. project management tools.

The system inventory can usefully record basic information about:

- when the system was developed, who developed it, development effort spent, when its next upgrade is due;
- development environment and development tools used;
- execution environment (online/batch proportions, number of clients/servers, hardware platform, database, etc.);
- some view of its size (any readily available metrics can be used, for instance number of windows, batch jobs, tables, function points, business processes supported, business objects);
- a view of its technical quality, in terms of error rates and the cost of correcting errors, the quality of its documentation, and the quality of its design. In terms of design, it is useful to identify how easily it would lend itself to componentization. Does it have a well-structured, layered design or not? Is the processing of different business events separate or intertwined? How easy would it be to separate business objects?

It is useful to record which parts of the organization use the system, through online access, reports, or extract files. Numbers of users, locations of use, transaction throughput, database volumes, number of complaints when the system is not available, number of change requests, and other such information can help identify the significance of the system and to whom it is significant.

It is also useful to cross-reference the component blueprint with each system, indicating which business processes are supported by each system and which business objects are used. Is the system one that embeds competitive advantage, or is it a standard business application? What is the level of requirement for change and the urgency of those requirements?

A detailed audit of a system will cover the same kinds of issues as a high-level inventory, but is likely to consider them in more detail. It is also likely to focus on an investigation of particular change requirements and possible strategies for addressing them.

7.3.2   Evaluating the relevance of componentization

The purpose of this task is to identify which current systems might particularly benefit from componentization. It is particularly relevant for systems that:

- are key to business success; and
- are subject to high levels of change; or
- have a current need for renovation or replacement.

For these systems, componentization is particularly relevant where there is a high level of duplication between systems, especially if this duplication is associated with high maintenance costs and requirements for duplication of changes. (Opportunities for reuse should not be the prime motivator for the decision as to where to focus development effort.)

Based on the ease of componentization (which is dependent on the design of the existing system) and the requirements for change, the best strategy for each application may be to:

- leave the application or parts of it uncomponentized (appropriate where there is little requirement for change);
- create components by wrapping legacy code (appropriate where an application is well architected but changes are required);
- build or buy new components (appropriate where significant change is required and the existing application is either not well architected or not of good quality).

Where new components are required, it is relevant to consider whether to build in-house, outsource the development, or buy a package or relevant components (assuming these are available). This decision is likely to be affected by factors such as:

- time-to-market – urgent requirements may sometimes best be met by a buy decision;
- business domain and technical knowledge – are these most likely to be found in-house (this is likely for areas of competitive advantage) or with outsourcers?

Componentization is not relevant for existing systems that meet current business requirements and do not require change, except where they may be scavenged for components to be used elsewhere.

7.4   Establishing an architectural framework

As part of creating an initial CBD strategy, we also need to define the technological framework we will use for components, covering the software architecture and infrastructure issues that were outlined in Chapter 5. This framework covers aspects that will apply across all projects within the scope of the component adoption initiative.

Aspects that need to be covered include:

- defining the technical environment;
- defining the software infrastructure, including definition of development standards;
- selecting or defining the component model to be used.

An architectural framework tends to evolve over time and one important aspect of managing it is to make it explicit, so that areas requiring attention become more evident.

7.4.1   Technical environment

The definition of the technical environment should include:

- platforms to be used;
- technologies to be used on each platform – language, component model/ component execution environment, middleware, runtime technology, security;
- component types and software infrastructure to be placed on each platform and technologies to be used for them, including definition of how components will interoperate (transport and protocol);
- notes on how isolation of technology-specific aspects is achieved (where action is required to achieve this);
- planned communication paths between platforms;
- failover, load balancing, recovery, use of replicated servers;
- notes on platforms to be phased out and new technologies to be adopted.

Some aspects of the technical environment can be defined once, as guidelines that apply in all cases. Other aspects, such as the placing of components on particular platforms, are likely to require definition as new applications are developed.

To mitigate problems with interoperability between components built using different technologies or to run on different platforms, it is desirable to select a restricted range of technologies for use, so as to reduce technical incompatibilities and inconsistencies. Technology-dependent aspects are best handled in a way that has as good a potential for upward compatibility as can reasonably be achieved without second-guessing future developments.

Figure 7.2 shows a sample technical environment that might have evolved over time.

It is the task of the technical architecture to explain, for this environment, what client platform should be used for different user groups or different purposes, what development software and layers of the application architecture should be implemented on each platform, and how technology-specific aspects are to be isolated.

7.4.1.1   *Selection of component execution environment*

Selection of the component execution environment is a key decision that may predetermine to a large extent both:

● the software infrastructure; and

● the set of component types to be used (i.e. component model).

7.4.2   Software infrastructure and development standards

Parts of the work of developing an application can be standardized and handled by a software infrastructure, potentially with associated code generation. This reduces development effort and simplifies the application developer's task. For a component-based architecture, the software infrastructure can be provided in the form of a component framework that handles standardized aspects of component behavior.

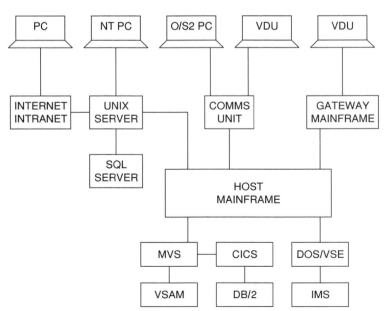

Figure 7.2
A sample technical environment

Software infrastructure definition should cover the aspects outlined in Section 5.3 on page 63. It involves:

- defining development standards;

- identifying opportunities for generating parts of the software from model-based definitions of components, e.g. for generating standard user interface components for simple CRUD (create, read, update, delete) type applications or for generating standard data access modules;

- identifying whether software infrastructure requirements can be met by the component execution environment, whether software or frameworks could be bought to meet some requirements, or whether custom-built software would be useful.

7.4.2.1   Interoperability standards

How do you handle interoperability between components developed using different technologies? It is desirable to have a consistent approach, and therefore a standard. However, such a standard should be concrete. The best way to produce a concrete standard is usually to define it on an "as-needs" basis in the context of a specific requirement as it is easy to flounder when asked to produce something abstract that you do not expect to have to use yourself.

Prototyping is often required to determine the best way to manage an interface between components developed using different technologies. Following production of a prototype, a standard solution can be documented that explains:

- architectural constraints and strategies to be adopted, e.g. limits on the scope of transactions;

- how an adapter component is to be coded;

- whether an adapter can be generated;

- how communications protocols/software are to be used, where relevant.

7.4.3   Component model

The component model can be viewed as defining an architectural style. It defines the type of building block, or component, that will be used to build an application, and constraints on how components of different types can be connected. It also describes how software infrastructure and business-related software domains interrelate, and the relationships between software components in the different domains, e.g. the use of a layered or other architecture.

The chosen component execution environment predetermines to a large extent the set of component types to be used. Within any constraints imposed by the choice of component execution environment, the organization's component model should define:

- the domains that make up an application and are used to separate different aspects of a software system;

- the types of component that can be defined in each domain and how these can be combined into larger components that combine logic from more than one domain;
- how components in one domain may interact with those in another domain, for instance by defining a layered architecture;
- types of component within a domain and how components of the different types may interact.

The considerations involved in defining a component model are discussed in Chapter 6.

7.5   Organizational considerations

The development organization itself may require changes in order to adapt to CBD. The key issues that need to be reviewed are as follows.

- How to introduce a component-based approach and disseminate understanding of CBD. One aid to achieving this may be the introduction of a center of excellence for components.
- Who will carry out the planning activities required for CBD.
- How the development organization is partitioned into groups or teams. Will these teams enable or hinder the introduction of components? Are there duplications between teams?
- Whether it is desirable to split the development organization between component developers and component assemblers.
- How technical architecture issues are handled. Should there be a separate technical architecture group? Is a team needed to develop the technical infrastructure?
- How component assets will be cataloged and managed.

These organizational issues are discussed further in Chapter 9.

7.6   Program planning

I assume a model of CBD in which development activities are undertaken only when there are firm commercial reasons why those activities are required. A visionary attempt to launch a development project that has the objective of redeveloping the whole application portfolio as a set of components simply for the sake of it is unlikely to receive funding. Indeed, such an approach would be very unlikely to provide benefits to compensate for its risks, unless there are exceptional circumstances.

Instead, program planning identifies where development effort is required and schedules the identified activities. The purpose of program planning is to define a development schedule, based on current requirements for business applications, which takes into account the planned direction defined in the component blueprint and the current situation as assessed during the audit of current assets. The objective is to ensure that the planned development activities move the organization's application portfolio toward a sounder, more component-based architecture.

Program planning itself is a standard activity that is carried out in a modified form when a component-based approach is adopted. It involves the following.

1 Assessing development priorities to determine what development projects should be undertaken. This assessment is based on current business needs and problems.

2 Determining how these development needs can best be met by evaluating how current systems meet the needs, and how best to move the application portfolio toward a component-based architecture. A feasibility study may be required in order to decide the best approach. Options to consider are:

 – maintenance with no reengineering, i.e. modifying the software to meet new business requirements without any attempt to improve the level of componentization. This may be appropriate, depending on the changes required;

 – reengineering or wrapping existing software. This may be appropriate where software that requires changes offers good potential for componentization, as revealed by the audit of current assets, particularly if the software, once componentized, can be used to eliminate redundancy in the software portfolio;

 – replacing the existing software with componentized software. Redundant software that is earmarked for replacement by other existing software can be replaced at the point in time at which changes are needed;

 – purchase of a new component or package. This may be the best choice if any of the following are true: the requirement is not met by the current application portfolio; the cost of reengineering the existing software is too high; or there are reasons for moving on from the technology used by the existing software;

 – development of a new component. This may be the choice where a suitable new component for purchase cannot be found, or is not likely to be found, or where the component would provide competitive advantage or require special tailoring to the company's needs.

3 Componentization is particularly relevant to consider in areas where redundancy or inconsistency have been identified in the current application portfolio. Once a componentized version of such software has been produced, other redundant versions can be replaced when they next require significant change, or earlier if the cost of maintenance or the business benefits of consistency justify this.

4 Where component framework requirements have been identified, the activity to develop the component framework should be scheduled as part of program planning.

5 Where the development strategy has identified a need to develop or reengineer a number of components, it may be worth considering whether a separate team should be set up to develop these, or whether an existing team should take on the task.

Some of the issues the program planner faces when trying to move the application portfolio forward are discussed in the next chapter.

8 Pragmatics of program planning

This chapter discusses how a component-based approach can be put into effect over time, as part of program planning. How do you reconcile the ideal vision with the messy reality?

It covers the management of some specific problem issues:

- dealing with legacy applications;
- dealing with packages;
- managing procurement issues, e.g. handling the outsourcing relationship.

Managing ownership and reuse issues within the organization is also an issue that affects program planners. This topic was discussed in Chapter 4.

8.1   Application integration and renewal

Legacy applications must form an integral part of every organization's application portfolio. This section explains why this is so and introduces strategies for application renewal that make it possible to move an organization's application portfolio forward gradually, with fewer complete rewrites of existing applications.

I use the term "legacy" to refer to existing applications that do not have the maintainability and flexibility that we seek to achieve with component-based applications.

8.1.1   Why legacy applications are here to stay

It is simply not realistic to redevelop the entire portfolio of applications that has been built up over an extended period of time. It costs too much, there are not enough IT staff to do it, and we have learned through hard experience that large-scale redevelopment projects have a low chance of success due to their complexity. These factors generally outweigh any business benefits from redevelopment, as well as the available budget.

We have to live with the fact that any organization's application portfolio will consist of existing applications and newly developed applications, and that these must coexist and interoperate. Moreover, this is not just a temporary situation, but something that we have to recognize as part and parcel of the problem space we deal with as software developers.

Our approach to upgrading applications, or adapting to new technologies, cannot usually be to recommend a big-bang approach that requires all systems to be migrated at once to any new technology.

8.1.2   How to manage legacy applications

Given that legacy applications are here to stay, we must consider how best to manage this situation. How can we ensure that our application portfolio can accommodate the kind of changes that the business requires?

Obviously, new applications we build should reuse existing application logic where possible to avoid redundancy. And any new application we build will have to be integrated with existing applications, exchanging data as necessary. Integration will be a major issue, not just for applications we develop ourselves but also for packages we purchase. The potential to integrate the package successfully is likely to be key when deciding to purchase.

If we adopt the most obvious, directly technical, approach to reusing legacy applications, there is a risk that the new systems we build will immediately suffer from the same problems of inflexibility as some of our existing ones. To see the danger more clearly, suppose that we evolve our applications based on the shape they already have, without giving much consideration to how the existing application fits into the overall picture.

To address new business requirements we often find we need to create a new application by building a new application front end that interfaces with business logic contained in an existing application. The most obvious approach would be to define interfaces to the legacy application at the points at which the structure of the legacy application makes interfaces possible. The simplest approach merely structures the new application front end in such a way that it can use these interfaces. See Figure 8.1 for a depiction of this approach.

This makes the structure of the application front end dependent on the practicalities of interfacing with the legacy application. Because of our approach, we will probably also build into the application front end whatever knowledge it needs about the physical implementation of the legacy application in order for it to function. This means that the application front end we would build for a different implementation of the same business logic would have to be different.

This approach limits the potential for moving the application portfolio forward. It has a number of deficiencies.

1   The new application front end is likely to build in knowledge of the existing application's design. It is exposed to any deficiencies that the existing

Figure 8.1
Reusing a legacy
application

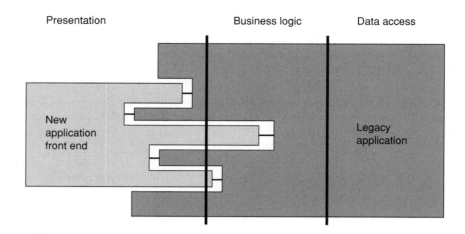

Presentation   Business logic   Data access

New application front end

Legacy application

application's design may suffer from. It does not separate concerns, so that the impact of any change is likely to be spread between new and old code in an unpredictable way. Any person carrying out maintenance will need to understand both the new and the legacy application in order to make changes.

2 We have allowed the location of easy interface points to determine the structure of our new application. This is unlikely to result in a good maintainable architecture.

3 We have built a local solution. We have done nothing to move the application portfolio as a whole toward more reusable components, with a reduction in redundancy, etc. It is unlikely that the misshapen components we have now produced will be reusable in other contexts. The result of our work offers no improved potential for rearchitecting the original legacy application.

A more structured approach to reusing and reengineering legacy code, on the other hand, can help improve the level of componentization of the application portfolio, with all the benefits that this brings.

To achieve this, we can aim to give the new application an architecture that is not based on the structure of existing legacy code but on the requirements of the new application. We can design the application's architecture to fit in with the overall architecture toward which we aim to move the application portfolio as a whole. Our target architecture, in terms of core business logic, is represented by the component blueprint.

By building in terms of the components that we wish to have in the long term, even if we implement these components only partially, we move the architecture of the application portfolio in the planned direction. Our new components will "wrap" the interfaces with the legacy application. They have the shape and scope we want for future use. They also present a standard interface to the outside world, so that exposure to the idiosyncrasies of the legacy application is reduced.

Figure 8.2 shows an example of the use of wrapper components.

It is also important to ensure that the part of the resulting application that is "exposed" to the legacy application is minimized. Knowledge of the particular programing details of the legacy application should be restricted to the wrapping component and to as small a part of the wrapper as possible. This makes the impact of changes more predictable and reduces the amount of code we have to inspect in order to make a change safely.

While the wrapper components themselves remain unavoidably exposed to the legacy application, the extent of this exposure has been reduced. Moreover, we now have an upgrade path. We can reuse the components we have created in contexts other than those from which they were taken, since they were created with a scope and purpose that is in accordance with our component strategy.[1] This contrasts with the lack of reuse potential offered by the approach I described previously.

We are now also in a position to upgrade legacy applications opportunistically. When changes are required to one business component, we may decide to achieve this by full reengineering of the part of the business logic for which the legacy application is still responsible, removing the requirement for the legacy application to be present when the component is used.

While some existing applications are likely to have areas in which they duplicate one another, that duplication can also be eliminated in an opportunistic way over a period of time, whenever duplicated functionality for which a component is now available requires change.

Gradually, we can migrate to a better architected application portfolio. As the application portfolio becomes better architected, its ability to respond to change improves. One particular benefit is that we can create or replace a component

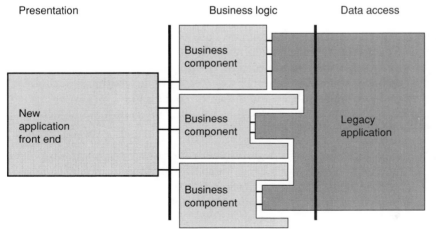

Figure 8.2
Wrapping a legacy application[2]

1. Note that the wrapper components will not necessarily be business components. Application components and data access components may also wrap legacy code.
2. They do of course still require the legacy code in order to function.

Figure 8.3
Gradual migration to a
component-based
application portfolio

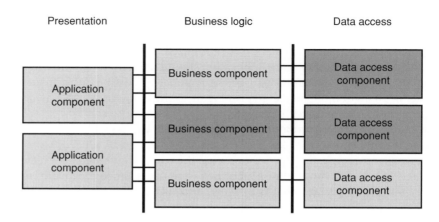

more easily than we could create or replace whole applications, thus reducing the extent to which the portfolio of legacy code slows our speed of response.

Thus, this planned approach to application renewal gives us a way of managing legacy applications that produces over time a greater degree of consistency and integration between applications. It gives us a strategy that allows legacy applications and component-based applications to coexist for an extended period of time. It assists in developing a strategy such that legacy applications can be gradually replaced by components, producing a more integrated application portfolio with less redundancy.

The ultimate result of the gradual migration process will be a component-based application portfolio, as illustrated in Figure 8.3.

8.2   Integrating packages

Packages present integration problems both because they are fixed entities and because packages are generally currently not well componentized. Some packages are moving toward improved componentization, but most package vendors face the same problems as the rest of us – a legacy of monolithic application code that is poorly componentized and difficult to maintain.

Specific integration issues related to handling integration with packages can be summarized as follows.

- The means provided for integration with the package. Application programming interfaces may be provided, or batch file interfaces, or it may be necessary to integrate at the data level through database access. The means of integration offered and the interfaces offered probably won't exactly match the interfaces of components in the component blueprint, with the result that wrapping of the interfaces to the package is likely to be desirable.

- Duplication of functionality between the package and other parts of the application portfolio. These should be eliminated as far as possible, but it may be necessary to accept some duplication. If there is duplication, there may be a need to synchronize data between the different systems. In this case, it is desirable to make sure only one system creates and updates any particular item of data (e.g. customer information) while the other systems only read that data. It may be necessary to partition responsibilities for different attributes of the same record, so that one system has overall responsibility for creation and deletion of records of a given type, but another updates some specific attributes.

8.3   Outsourcing

Outsourcing presents a different sort of problem. More control over the application to be developed is possible than with a package, making it easier to ensure that applications do integrate as required. Anyway, the logistics of outsourcing make it desirable that the software to be developed has as few interfaces with other software as possible, so that the need for communication is decreased and this can fit well with a component-based approach.

It is desirable that the outsourcer should agree to conform to company standards, using software infrastructure as required to fit into the overall architecture, and developing components that fit into the component blueprint. However, from the outsourcer's point of view, such requirements make it more difficult to cost an item of work. The outsourcer is also likely to fear, sometimes correctly, that the company's architecture may not be well defined, making it difficult to quantify effort or guarantee delivery on schedule.

Internal political issues can arise where software development is outsourced. If a business department is authorized to commission its own applications and chooses to build its applications in-house, the in-house development organization is in a position to consider how the application fits into the overall application portfolio and may see opportunities for reuse. However, if the application is outsourced, then ensuring that the outsourcer takes into account the customer's application portfolio as a whole when designing the application depends on the business department's willingness to accept this as a requirement.

9 Organization for component-based development

This chapter discusses alternative organizational structures for implementing a CBD program. It also discusses roles and team structures for strategy planning, component acquisition, and component assembly.

9.1   Organizing development with components

One of the greatest assets of an organization is the knowledge that team members acquire over a period of time. For this reason, it makes sense to develop a relatively static organization that allows team members to acquire depth of understanding in particular areas of expertise. It is true that a relatively static organization has also to cater for individuals' needs, allowing them to move between roles or groups, so that they can stay interested and avoid becoming stale.

Some of the expertise required by developers is specifically technical, but in a business environment much of the relevant knowledge relates to an understanding of the business and of the type of application required by a particular part of the business.

Given a component blueprint, it should be relatively easy to define a development organization that allocates different components, or sets of components, to different teams. Here are some considerations that are relevant to organizing for CBD, particularly with respect to the division of work between different teams.

9.1.1   Center of excellence

Especially when introducing a component-based approach, it can be useful to have a separate center of excellence for CBD. Individuals in this team are responsible for building up a special understanding of the topic. Such a team often works well as a body that sets standards and reviews results. It may also help by maintaining a component catalog and advising on available components. It should not, in my view, be a development center itself.

It is desirable for team members to spend some time participating in individual development projects. This can be helpful in:

- preventing members of the central team from losing touch with the real world and also ensuring that they get feedback as to how usable the products of the central team are in practice;
- ensuring that individual project teams are aware of the assets that are available for reuse through the presence of a team member who is motivated to bring these assets to the team's attention;
- circulating among other staff the design expertise with components that the center of excellence acquires.

A large center of excellence is not usually helpful. It runs the risk of becoming over-bureaucratic, producing standards that are never used, or of itself moving actively into component development. If the center of excellence does move into component development, it runs the risk of causing political problems through infringement of the territories of the development teams, with resultant demotivation.

9.1.2   Separation of component development and component assembly

One model that is often proposed for component development is one in which one set of developers develops components, and a different part of the organization assembles these components into applications.

This approach offers advantages.

- It helps ensure that components are well defined and truly separable. Where the same developer is responsible for developing components and assembling them, there is a likelihood that the resulting components will turn out to be tightly coupled with hidden dependencies. Where the assembler of the components is not the developer, the component developer must pay greater attention to making sure the components really are well defined.
- It can make it possible for component developers and component assemblers to develop different specialisms.

There can be a useful split between teams that are allocated parts of the business domain and focus on developing business components, and teams that focus on producing applications to meet specific requirements. However, in my view, the teams that deliver applications are not restricted to the role of being mere application assemblers. On the contrary, their role in producing an application that meets the customer's requirements is key. The presentation layer is also not usually assembled from pre-existing components but is built for the specific application and therefore requires development skills.

There is a risk that components developed in isolation will be developed with too much of an idealistic focus, with too little attention to actual requirements, costing more effort and ultimately failing to meet requirements. Completely separating application project teams from component development teams is a risky choice for an organization with little experience of CBD, because of the lack of individuals with the skills and experience required either to manage the process or to define and develop components.

When starting out with CBD, and arguably even once experience has been acquired, it is usually better to focus the organization around application development projects in which both component development and solution assembly are part of the same application development project. There may usefully be separate teams developing the business components and the application components, but both types of team are under common management working toward delivery of a specific project.

Over time, the teams responsible for delivering business components may be able to take on an independent role, responding to requirements from project teams to deliver new and modified components, and servicing the needs of more than one application development project.

Ultimately, the importance of delivery dates means that individual application projects must usually be in a position to require that any teams they depend on do deliver to their requirements and their timescales. This means that development must usually be driven from the individual application projects.

Separate component development teams can be important when individual projects are so heavily focussed on meeting deadlines in a short period of time that components which will benefit the organization in the longer term cannot be adequately engineered within the bounds of individual application development projects. In this case, the longer-term strategic initiative has to be decoupled at least from short-term delivery dates, and the task of developing the strategic components may be given to a separate team. It is inadvisable, however, to leave any team without a real delivery date, or without a milestone that is less than six months away. There should be a concrete plan as to where and how the results of the "strategic" development effort are to be used. Ultimately, this means that even such strategic initiatives should be bound in with, and managed with, a planned application development project.

9.1.3 Application project-based component development

Each individual application project will involve some or all of the following:

- use of business components, and maybe of application components, that have been developed by other teams;
- a need to develop new business components and data access components;
- the building of new application components for this specific application;
- assembling of the application, including integration with existing legacy applications, the building of bridges (adapters) between existing components, and the building of business-to-business interfaces;

● identification of requirements for improvements or changes to the software infrastructure or component framework.

The development of business and data access components and their assembly can usefully be split between two teams on the same project, but this is not always necessary, depending on team size and skills.

Both developing components and assembling them within a single project team creates a risk that components will not be truly well designed and separable, but will be built such that there are unintended dependencies between the different components that will obstruct maintainability. One way of mitigating this risk is to ensure that a developer who works on one component does not also develop any component that acts as a client to, or provides services to, that component. It is always important to review the interfaces of the component to ensure that the design is good. This becomes particularly important if there is reason to suspect that the link between component producer and component assembler might be too close.

9.1.4   Technical architecture and infrastructure

There are some similarities in terms of organizational issues between developing a technical infrastructure and the development of core business components. Often, initial thoughts on technical infrastructure requirements emerge from individual application projects.

For any organization with a significant amount of software, it will become necessary to handle technical infrastructure development as a separate project, and most probably as a strategic project that is not expected to deliver fully in the short timescales of current, time-critical application projects. At the same time, technical infrastructure developments should, like component development, be clearly targeted at use in individual application projects, and some of these will be short term and tactical.

For a significant application development, there could be a technical infrastructure team within an overall application project team, with the resulting technical infrastructure being carried forward for use in other projects, probably by a core technical infrastructure team that becomes separate from the individual application project teams.

9.2   Organizing planning

This section briefly outlines some of the roles that are important during the planning process. See Table 9.1.

Once the component blueprint has been established, a feedback loop is needed. There are two points at which this feedback loop is used:

● as part of the process of establishing the specification for a particular component assembly project. The set of components defined should be checked

Table 9.1   Key roles during the planning process

Task	Who to involve
Defining the scope and expected benefits of the CBD initiative	This is likely to be directly controlled by the sponsor of the initiative and any manager appointed to oversee the initiative, with results agreed with the management team as a whole
Defining a component blueprint	This is best carried out by the senior analysts or architects responsible for the business functionality provided for different business areas
Auditing current systems	This can be carried out by senior analysts or designers who have a good understanding of good design practice. Since reviewing one's own work is not usually a good idea, audits should usually be carried out by a group that was not involved in the original development
Establishing an architectural framework	A chief technical architect, or technical architecture group, should establish the architectural framework. There may be an IT-wide technical architecture group, or – in start-up cases – there may be a chief architect who works with individual project teams to develop an architectural framework that can be improved from project to project
Organization	Defining the organization is a task for management
Program planning	This is a management task that is usually carried out with the assistance of senior analysts who carry out feasibility studies, etc.

against the component blueprint and accepted or rejected, with the component blueprint being updated if appropriate;

● at the end of the delivery process, when the components produced should be verified and checked against the component blueprint.

In order to carry out this activity, there should be a custodian, or custodians, of the component blueprint who can monitor progress and ensure that projects do, in fact, make progress toward the production of the planned set of components rather than toward chaos.

This is a quality control role, which requires a high level of understanding of how components are best defined, as well as a willingness to accept valid suggestions for improvements. It is a role that can usefully be divided between the senior analysts or architects who have responsibility for a particular business area, and are the ultimate custodians of the business functionality, and experts in component-based design who may be members of a center of excellence.

9.3   Organizing component acquisition and assembly

This section outlines some of the roles involved in component acquisition and assembly, together with a possible set of groupings. Teams need team leaders, and for each type of role there may be one person who takes the lead (e.g. chief architect, lead analyst, etc.). This is not spelt out in Table 9.2. There may also be separate developer roles in some environments, such as designer, developer, and tester. These are not referred to in the table except where they play a special role in CBD.

Table 9.2   Roles in component acquisition and assembly

Group/Role	Description
Business architecture	
Business analysts	Each business analyst, or architect, is responsible for business requirements for a particular part of the business. It is useful to have business analysts who are responsible for a specific business unit's requirements. There may also be a need for business analysts who are responsible for areas that are of interest to multiple business units
Technical architecture	
Technical architect	Is responsible for the overall technical vision. He or she is not directly involved in development but operates as a direction setter and a reviewer. There may be only one technical architect or there may be a small group of technical architects
Technical infrastructure team(s)	
Infrastructure developers	Develop the technical infrastructure or a part of it. Good technical programing skills are required, with a solid understanding of the base technologies used and an understanding of what forms part of an infrastructure as opposed to being business-related logic. The role requires good collaborative skills and a willingness to accept other development teams, or other developers, as the customer

(continued)

Table 9.2 *Continued*

Group/Role	Description
Business component development team	
Component developers	Develop business components and data access components. Require a strong understanding of the business logic of the relevant business domain and good abstract thinking capabilities to enable development of components that separate concerns and will be usable in multiple contexts
Application development team	
Application analyst/designer	Evaluates alternative ways of sourcing components (reuse, buy, or build), usually as part of a separate project phase before the solution assembly project kicks off
Application developers	Develop application components and assemble applications. Require user interface design skills and knowledge of user interface programing, as well as a strong understanding of usability factors, the application area, and the customer's needs
Application assemblers	An optional specialist role for developers who build adapters or legacy wrappers
Component management team	or CBD center of excellence. Members of this team are likely to combine some of the following roles
Component catalog manager/librarian	Manages the component catalog
Component standards manager	Creates component-related standards and advises on CBD
Component blueprint guardian	Reviews components that are created to ensure that they conform to the component blueprint, with changes necessary to the component blueprint being agreed with the business analysts

Building and assembling components

Acquiring components 10

Using an existing component, rather than developing a new one, is often – though not always – the quickest and (or) cheapest method of meeting any given need. An existing component could be bought or it could be procured within the organization. If a suitable component cannot be acquired, it may be possible to modify an existing component. Otherwise, the component will have to be developed from scratch, which is often the slowest and most costly route, though it is the most likely way of meeting requirements exactly.

Most software that can be purchased either takes the form of a software package, and so is too large to qualify as a component, or is a widget, user interface control, or other software component that is too small to qualify as a component, at least in terms of my definition of what a component is. Currently, there is not a large market in components, so that consideration of purchasing a component may still be a rather theoretical topic.[1] However, you should still consider purchasing a software package since cost and speed of delivery often override the pursuit of a purely component-based portfolio, despite the merits of the latter.

Purchasing a component is similar to evaluating a component within an organization but is likely to require a more formal process. When procuring an existing component, there is usually an expectation that the component should be usable "as-is". However, modifications may be necessary and negotiable. Equally, in-house, if no component is available to use "as-is", it may be possible to modify software that the organization already possesses.

Clearly, the length of an evaluation exercise should bear some relation to the value of the component being acquired. It would not usually be worth acquiring

---

1. There are organizations engaged in making components available, including larger business-sized components. See, for instance, www.componentsource.com

a component if the cost in effort of the evaluation exceeded the cost of developing the component from scratch. And when evaluating alternative options, it is desirable that the effort spent making the choice should not exceed the potential benefit to be gained by making the better choice. Over-zealous evaluators sometimes need to be reminded of these points!

10.1   Shortlisting components

10.1.1   Looking for components

Potential suppliers can be identified through market awareness, through the Internet and trade literature, or through specialist consultants. When looking for a package, a wider range of potential suppliers is likely to be available than when looking for a component.

To keep evaluations manageable, it is useful to limit long lists to 6–8 suppliers, while including 2–4 alternatives in a shortlist and subjecting only one candidate to detailed gap analysis.

10.1.2   Screening candidate components

Screening criteria help eliminate candidates to reduce a list of candidate components to a manageable size. Relevant items to consider are:

- basic fit with application requirements;
- whether the software runs on the required platform and is compatible with other software that is to be used;
- the vendor's characteristics – is support available, will the vendor survive, is source code available if the vendor does not survive?
- how easy it is to customize the software, where relevant.

For a component, its ability to run within your component execution environment is a key consideration.

10.1.3   Formal evaluations

Usually, a formal evaluation will only be appropriate when purchasing a package. For a component, because it is smaller, a much briefer, informal evaluation makes sense.

When selecting a software package, vendors on a longlist could be asked to respond to a Request for Information (RFI), while vendors on a shortlist are asked to respond to a Request for Proposal (RFP). These ask questions concerning:

- the software's coverage of requirements, relating to both business functionality and technical requirements, including integration requirements;
- the vendor's details, including financial information;
- details of product plans;

- costs, licensing model, contractual details;
- reference customers;
- handling of implementation of the product (customization, installation, data migration, user documentation, training);
- support and maintenance.

Scoring mechanisms can be used to evaluate the responses. Two possible scoring mechanisms are:

1 A simple Yes/No scoring grid with knock-out criteria identified. Each vendor is scored by adding up the number of Yes answers. A vendor is eliminated if there is a No to any knock-out question. (Obviously, you do not let the vendors know which are the knock-out criteria.) This is usually the best scoring approach for an RFI.

2 A weighted evaluation mechanism, described below. Because weightings are, by definition, subjective, weighted scores should always be presented beside the unweighted scores so that it is clear what effect the weightings have.

It can be useful to produce separate scores for each level of priority of the requirements, as identified during requirements capture. Priorities could be, for instance:

A Essential for initial implementation
B Essential, but a temporary workaround exists
C Significant benefit, difficult to achieve another way
D Significant benefit, an alternative is available.

10.1.3.1 Weighted evaluation mechanism

One way of allocating weightings is as follows.

- Identify broad evaluation categories and allocate percentages to each category.
- Subdivide each category and divide 100 percent between the subcategories of each category.
- For functionality, a simple Yes/No scoring system at use case or business service level, with a score of 1 for Yes and 0 for No, can work well as each use case or business service should be of roughly the same size. An alternative is to subdivide percentages between different business processes, based on their relative importance, and subdivide that percentage between use cases or user task components.
- You could adjust the score by awarding more points for currently available functionality than for functionality available via modifications or for functionality currently in Beta test. (It is best to ignore planned functionality that is not yet in Beta test.) Alternatively, you can score separately to show the degree of fit without modifications, the degree of fit with modifications, and the degree of fit with the next release – or simply choose to ignore all non-current functionality (usually the safest practice).

Table 10.1 shows an example of a scoring grid.

Table 10.1 Example of a scoring grid

No.	Criterion	Percent	Weight	Score	Weighted score
1	Interfaces	40			
2	Functionality	40			
3	Non-functional requirements	20			
1.1	...				
2.1	Order entry	40	16	1	16
2.2	Invoicing	40	16	1	16
2.3	Stock control	20	8	0	0
3.1	...				

At each level of decomposition, 100 percent is allocated amongst the items within the category. These percentages are multiplied by the percentage allocated to the category as a whole to obtain a weighting that can be applied to the score.

10.1.4 Reference visits

A reference site visit can be used to check up on points where RFP responses were not clear or convincing, or to check on other key issues that were identified during the evaluation process.

A reference site visit can be particularly useful as a way of determining the level of assistance the vendor's staff have been able to offer and the ease of implementation of the software, for instance the length of time taken to implement it and the problems encountered during the process.

10.1.5 Selecting a candidate

As a result of this preliminary evaluation, one candidate component or package can be selected for detailed analysis of its fit, with possible replacement candidates if the selected component fails the more detailed analysis.

At this stage, it will be known how close the competition is. This will make it possible to decide, subsequently, whether drawbacks that are discovered later in the selected candidate should cause any of the other alternatives to be reconsidered.

10.2   Assessing fit and specifying changes

10.2.1 Assessing fit

Gap analysis can be used to assess how well a component or software package meets requirements (Figure 10.1). It is used to evaluate:

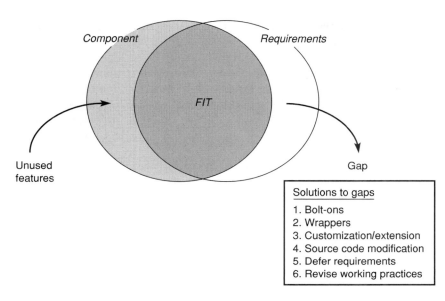

Figure 10.1
Assessing component fit

- the capabilities of the software that is the subject of the evaluation;
- the extent to which those capabilities match the stated business requirements;
- the effort required to modify the software to meet requirements;
- whether an alternative would be to adapt work practices to fit with the work practices supported by the component or package.

The length of time to give to the evaluation depends on what the alternatives are seen to be. Clarifying the decision criteria in advance can help avoid time being wasted on evaluations that will have no effect on the outcome. For instance, if one concern is whether the component or software does in fact deliver the functionality that is claimed, or is reasonably error-free, then define how this will be checked. What is proof enough? It is undesirable as part of an evaluation to attempt to take over the job of the vendor's quality assurance department.

10.2.1.1   Technical characteristics

While in-house software may be taken on trust, for third-party software it is worth checking the software itself (but see previous section) to determine:

- whether the software/component does what the vendor says it does;
- how error-free the software is;
- support for required volumes, performance, recovery, or other relevant non-functional requirements.

10.2.1.2   Ease of reengineering

For a component that is to be reengineered from an existing application, the ease with which the component can be cut out from the existing application should be assessed. Does the application offer suitable entry points at which the required logic can be called?

Is the logic of the application intertwined such that logic that is needed is inseparable from logic that should not be included? If so, then a rewrite is effectively required and the software cannot be reused. This may be the case, for instance, where data access logic and business logic are intertwined making it impossible to extract data access logic, or where a module intertwines processing for multiple business functions making it difficult to extract the processing for the required function.

Are embedded commits incorporated in the software that make it difficult to extend the scope of commit units to provide required transactions? This may often be the case and code changes are likely to be necessary to address this.

Will interplatform communication mechanisms be required to allow use of the component on its own current platform? Or, as an alternative, will porting to a new platform be required?

10.2.1.3 Coverage of required business functionality

This involves mapping the functionality of the software or component to the required functionality, as documented in a requirements specification. At a superficial level, this is done at the longlist or shortlist stage, but it is desirable to limit more detailed investigation to a suitable candidate.

The evaluation should cover:

- interfaces into the component, the services it offers, and how these map to required functionality;
- for an application component, the extent to which the user interface mapping and workflow match that which is required. How good is the match with the organization's working practices?
- any events raised or consumed by the software;
- data managed by the component;
- the ability to customize to meet presentation, processing, or data management requirements.

10.2.2 Specifying changes

10.2.2.1 Reviewing gaps

Gaps and deficiencies are likely to be of the following main types.

- Functional mismatches – cases in which the functionality of the software does not match that which is required. Functionality may be missing, or business rules handled differently, or a different view taken of constraints. Software could also offer more functionality than is required – this is less of an issue as it may well be possible to simply not use the additional functionality.

- Data mismatches – cases where the application or component either requires data that the solution does not require or does not manage data that the solution does require. Where data coverage overlaps with that provided by existing software, can data be coordinated and kept synchronized? Is the data viewed in a compatible way?
- Technical issues – the platform may be wrong, or a different database used to that which is required, or the software may be difficult to componentize as required.

10.2.2.2   Options for resolving gaps

The options available will vary depending on whether the asset or component is to be purchased or not, and whether the source code is available for white-box modifications. Once options for resolving gaps have been identified, effort estimates are needed to help determine which option is the best to pursue.

Black-box customization
Black-box customization may be possible. For example:

- parameterization – a component or package may offer the option of setting parameters to customize the behavior of the software;
- bolt-ons – a component or package may allow customization through the use of user exits or hooks;
- customization interface – a component may offer special-purpose assembly services that allow controlled customization of a component, e.g. addition of code sections. A package may offer special-purpose assembly utilities to allow extension of the package, e.g. through the use of screen painters and report writers.

Customization points are discussed further in Chapter 11.

Non-intrusive modification
Non-intrusive modification can be achieved through the use of:

- wrappers – if the package or component offers services that can be invoked by another component, it may be possible to develop a wrapping component that offers the full services required. The wrapper extends the services of the wrapped component under the covers by invoking the services of the wrapped component but also adding additional functionality;
- adapters – these can be used to insulate two components from incompatibilities between them, e.g. format conversion.

Adaptation of working practices or requirements
If a requirement is not met by the software, one solution is to discard the requirement, or to postpone its implementation. If the software incorporates different working practices to those in use, it may be worth revising working practices rather than modifying the package to suit the current way of working.

Source code modification

There may be no alternative to white-box modification of the code in order to meet requirements. For existing application code, the ease with which gaps can be filled should be considered. Adding code at only a few well-defined points reduces to a minimum the extent to which the existing code must be modified, costs less, and is likely to be less error-prone. For software that is already in use, change control issues must also be considered.

It is often necessary to develop a new version of the component that may only later replace the old component in applications in which it is already used. In some cases, instead of creating a new version, a new component will be created by cloning and then modifying the component. This becomes necessary if the new component cannot accommodate both the existing and the new requirements, or sometimes where there are ownership issues.

For legacy applications, scavenging and reengineering may be required. (In principle, scavenging and reengineering could be used for software that is to be bought, but is it really worth buying software that fits requirements so poorly as to require this?)

Technical modifications

Possible types of modification include:

- porting to another platform;
- resolving technical issues raised by the use of multiple databases, data duplication, etc. Where feasible, modifying components to use the same database or to remove data redundancy provides the best solution to these issues;
- handling interoperability issues, through the use of adapters.

10.3   Acquiring the component

Having determined how to source the component, a business case must usually be made to get the necessary approval to acquire the component. The business case might include:

- a brief problem statement identifying the component or components to be acquired;
- a brief recommendation as to how the component or components should be acquired;
- an outline of key reasons for the choice made;
- a note on implications such as modifications required to the software or to current working practices, any disadvantages of the chosen solution, length of time to implement the solution;
- a calculation of the cost of purchase, showing the cost of purchase itself, the cost of any modifications required, the cost of installation, and the expected cost of maintenance and support;

- if it is relevant, a comparison of the case for acquisition via this route as compared with other options, e.g. comparative costs, the comparative benefits and disadvantages of the different possible acquisition methods, the risks of different routes, including the extent to which different acquisition methods progress or inhibit the overall CBD strategy.

11 Designing components

New components can be produced in a variety of ways. For instance, they can be built from scratch, "harvested" from existing legacy applications, or be existing components that are modified to meet new requirements.

For new development and for harvesting or reengineering existing legacy applications, the handling of a component development project is not radically different from that of a straightforward development project. Modification of components may be similar or may involve smaller-scale maintenance-type activities.

For the components that are to be developed or reengineered, possibly involving the wrapping of legacy code, the development process is fairly standard:

- analysis is required and a specification should be produced in the normal way;
- prototyping and design should be carried out;
- the components must be constructed and tested;
- the components can then be delivered to a solution assembly project or assembled by the same project team.

The main differences are as follows.

- Each individual component is relatively small. If different components were to be developed by separate teams, this would lead to very small teams and projects. As discussed in Part 2, it is more likely that a development project will develop more than one component at a time.
- Because some scoping of the components precedes the development project, some of the overall analysis will already have been done, and some of the

design issues will already have been resolved. Some of the activities that are usually included in a large-scale development project (e.g. selecting technical environment) will not be relevant, or can be carried out in a scaled-down form.

- Consideration of design for reuse assumes greater importance, as it is an objective to be able to reuse components in multiple contexts.
- Building in customization points becomes a possible requirement, particularly where it is the intention to sell components or to use them to build outsourced applications for more than one customer.
- It becomes important to consider how change will be handled.
- It becomes even more important than it is with a standard development project to build a regression test pack for each component that makes it possible to test the functioning of the component each time it is used in a new context.

This chapter aims to provide guidance on the following aspects that gain special importance with CBD:

- designing for reuse
- building customization points
- handling change
- creating components by wrapping existing software.

11.1   Designing for reuse

There are various quite different types of reuse that we could consider, only one of which is, in my opinion, intrinsically relevant to CBD. This is that a component should be designed such that the application can change around it without requiring that the component should change, unless it is the component's own function that is to be changed.

Another type of reuse that is certainly facilitated by the use of components is the ability to use the same component to perform a given function wherever that identical function is required. The small size of components as compared with applications facilitates this kind of reuse. This type of reuse, however, is a possible by-product of CBD. It is not, in my view, the yardstick to use when determining whether using components is yielding benefits.

There is a further type of reuse in which software reuse is achieved by making software more generic, abstracting away from differences in requirements between one situation and another, and attempting to use the generic module in multiple contexts. This is not necessarily a good practice, and is far too readily assumed by many practitioners to be the way reuse can be achieved.

Abstract, generic software has its uses, but it also has disadvantages.

- Such software is generally more complex, more difficult to understand, and more difficult to maintain.

- Generic components may require more development effort than context-specific counterparts.

- Generic components may involve a compromise on functionality, not providing all the features the customer requires.

- Generic software may perform more slowly than context-specific counterparts.

My preference is for a component blueprint that breaks down a problem space into components, each of which has its own specific purpose, such that the overall design reuses the component wherever its specific function is needed, rather than struggling to create generic components that will fail to meet requirements at the first change.

There is, of course, a place for generic code, but when it is required and valuable it is for reasons that are not related to the practice of CBD.

11.1.1   Generalizing for reuse

Having said that, however, understanding whether logic is common and can be reused or whether it is really different and should be handled separately is not entirely trivial. For example, there are any number of different accruals algorithms that can be used for calculating interest. The fact that they all relate to accrual might lead to the expectation that some reuse should be possible, but in fact, opportunities for reuse are likely to be limited as there are too many subtle variations.

It is also true that thinking of logic as distinct and separate can sometimes be too easy an option, where a more analytical approach would in fact discover ways to analyze problems that yield a separation between parts that are specific and parts that can be common.

The extent to which you invest effort in analyzing commonality will probably depend on the commercial opportunity that finding commonality would give you. An individual business only has to solve a problem once. A product vendor or software house, on the other hand, may have much more to gain from finding a design that provides a common solution to a problem, making its software development cheaper. This is why product vendors invest in understanding the commonality between different types of financial instrument, for instance, where each instrument may look different because of the different terminology that is used, but a common structure can be identified and built on.

Business logic could simply be common across the enterprise, so that no generalization is required. Where some parts are common and some aren't, there is a variety of ways in which reuse could be achieved.

- Defining supertypes and subtypes of business objects. To take an example, it may be that all accounts have characteristics and behavior in common. This common behavior can be handled in one place, with aspects of behavior that are specific to a particular type of account being separated out into specific components. The amount of common behavior must be reasonably significant before the additional complexity of this approach is justified, and such that you are confident that changes in one context will not impact what is thought of as being constant across the different uses.

- Generalization of logic. It may be that different parts of the business carry out similar activities with different variations. Discounting practices might differ, for instance. These differences in business practice range across the spectrum in terms of how intrinsic the differences are. Some differences may be intrinsic to the business and could not be dispensed with, while other differences are part of a particular business unit's way of doing business, and significant to those working in the area, but not intrinsic. Other differences may simply be habit – cosmetic choices that have little real impact. Given such variations, there are a number of possible approaches:

  - you could try to move the business toward a common approach;
  - you could try to simplify. Are all the bells and whistles really necessary? The cost of providing variations may outweigh their benefit and users may be willing to trade a costly minor benefit for something they would value more;
  - if these approaches are not possible, you could produce a generic solution with customization points, or exit points, to allow variations;
  - if all else fails, you will have to accept that the activities are, and will, remain different and require separate software.

I do not recommend designing for reuse in the abstract because it takes additional effort that may not be needed or available, is liable to error because the full requirements cannot be understood, and is almost doomed to failure given the future's habit of changing its mind about how it will look. Instead:

- generalize a component only if it is earmarked for use in more than one context, and then generalize only as much as is necessary for the envisaged applications;
- do not build in features you think you might need in the future;
- build based only on concrete requirements that you are able to obtain.

You can either build a component for two (or more) specific contexts for which you can obtain requirements, or you can aim to incorporate more uses through a process of revision as the component is reused. Here, analysts with in-depth understanding of the different contexts in which the component is likely to be used are invaluable in providing an understanding of what the key requirements will be.

11.1.2 Design principles affecting reuse

The key to designing components that will remain usable in the face of change is to scope them correctly. The issues involved were discussed in Chapter 6.

Here I summarize some key points.

- A component that is defined to fit into an overall conception or architecture has a much better chance of being reusable than one that is defined in an *ad hoc* manner.

- To be reusable, a component needs to be designed to be context-independent. The component should be designed in such a way that it can be put into a new context without dragging components that use it with it. Note that the component should not embody knowledge of how it is used. It offers a set of interfaces and services that is available to all users. I do not recommend designing a component to offer different sets of services to different users. (There will, of course, be logical groupings of services where the services in a group are likely to be used in combination to achieve a given end.)

- The component scope should include aspects that cannot be separated. If you have two mutually dependent components, question why you have two components and not one. The component should have a coherent purpose. (It should exhibit the traditional qualities of high cohesion and low coupling.)

- The services offered by a component should be context-independent. They should not be cast in a form that makes them aware of the context in which they are called. Think anthropomorphically. Try to define the services the component offers in terms of what the component could regard as its role and responsibilities, allowing it to reject any that do not strictly relate to the knowledge it necessarily incorporates. An *AllocateStock* service in a *Product* component is more use than a *FulfillOrder* service because stock could be allocated for other reasons than fulfilling an order, e.g. for allocating stock to a warehouse. If a component cannot reasonably exist without knowledge of other components, e.g. an *Order* cannot reasonably exist without a *Product* that is ordered, it is reasonable for it to know this and explicitly refer to products. Its knowledge should, however, be restricted to what it needs to know.

- Try to define each service so that it has a single purpose. It is better not to define a service that carries out additional processing simply in order to reduce the number of calls, as this reduces the chance of reuse. Multi-purpose services also increase maintenance costs, as any change could affect not just the changed function but also the other functions that have been bundled in, increasing the likelihood of error and the cost of testing.

- Keep the interface of a service small. Do not try to future-proof by adding parameters that are not currently needed. The future has a habit of changing.

- Name the service in a way that indicates clearly what it does. Although verb followed by object makes for more readable code, object followed by verb, e.g. *OrderFulfill*, makes it easier to find relevant services.

11.2   Building customization points

Components can be designed to be customizable at the time at which they are assembled into an application. The customization process may be one that involves hand coding on the part of the application developer, or may be one that is supported by an intelligent assembly environment.

To make it possible for an assembly environment to assist the application assembler with customization, the component generally needs to offer services that can be used by the assembly environment to enquire as to its capabilities, such as those that can be offered by JavaBeans or through the use of introspection. These services should be constructed in a standard way. Usually, it will not be worthwhile to build such an assembly environment and customization capabilities in-house (although some companies are doing this), and it will be better to wait until suitable development tools in this area mature.

The following represent some ways in which variation points can be provided.

11.2.1   Delegation

A reusable component is built that offers generalized services which can be used "as-is" in some cases, while in other contexts variant versions of the service will be required. To customize for a specific context, the developer builds a component that delegates requests to the reusable component where appropriate. The developer can decide:

- to handle a given request without invoking the corresponding service in the reusable component;
- to invoke the service in the reusable component but add extra logic before or after the invocation;
- to simply pass on the request to the reusable component.

11.2.2   Parameterization/extension points

In this case, the component offers:

- substitution parameters;
- sections of code to be completed or user exits to be supplied;
- alternative code sections which may be included or excluded based on options selected by the application assembler.

This type of variation point can be handled in a number of ways:

- a file may be used to contain parameter values;
- the component is presented as a white-box and the application assembler fills in the blanks;
- the application assembler is provided with details of possible user exits/bolt-ons, and supplies these using a standard development environment and traditional assembly procedures;

- the application assembler is presented with an interface at assembly time that allows the selection of the relevant options and completion of the relevant code.

11.2.3 Inheritance

A component can be defined with abstract or template services. (Abstract services have an interface but no implemented processing. Template services implement processing only by invoking abstract operations that the component does not implement.) To use the component, the application developer creates a component that inherits from the supplied component, and adds code for the abstract services/operations. To achieve this, you have, of course, to be using an environment that supports inheritance for components.[1]

Delegation can be used as a substitute for inheritance for environments that do not support inheritance. Even where inheritance is supported, delegation often provides a simpler, less error-prone approach.

11.3   Handling change

When a component is reused, handling of change becomes particularly critical. We do not want to have to revise and retest each application that uses a component when we change it. While retesting is a necessity (which should not cause problems if attention has been paid to producing repeatable regression tests), the extent to which existing applications must be revised if a component is changed can be substantially reduced.

Here is a summary of some of the options for defining interfaces in a way that ensures new versions of a component can be released without requiring all components that use it to be updated.

1   Components can be defined with immutable interfaces. When a change is made, a new interface must be defined. The component must guarantee that all existing interfaces will still work. This means that the updated component can be included in an application without any changes having to be made. Only those parts of the application that wish to use the facilities offered by the new interface have to be updated. This is the strategy used in Microsoft's COM component model. Note that this implies that services cannot be removed.

2   Interfaces could be self-describing. This can be achieved by using a tagged data format that precedes each data item with its name and format. XML is an example of this type of format. In this case, the user of a component can just retrieve parameters that are of interest and ignore other parameters. Obviously, the interface must not be upgraded in such a way as to impose change on existing users, e.g. by adding a mandatory argument.

1. This generally means an OO environment.

3 Interfaces can be described using meta-data. Another way of achieving self-describing interfaces is by storing meta-data in, for instance, a database or repository that describes the interface and is queried by the user of the component. Java reflection can be used in this way. XML schemas can also be used to provide this type of mechanism.

The first approach is the simplest. It can be used in combination with the other approaches so that any interface change that would force change on existing users is handled by defining a new interface instead.

The second and third approaches are more complicated and require infrastructure support if the coding effort of application assemblers is not to be increased. These approaches make it easier to plug together components that were not designed with each other in mind.

Another rather obvious point when changing components is that the nature of a service should remain constant. Do not attempt to subvert an existing service to make it capable of carrying out some new, different function. Instead, add a new service for the new function. (As I explained earlier, I am an opponent of multi-purpose services.)

11.4   Wrapping existing software

The basic principle of a wrapper is that it *fully replaces* the used component from the point of view of the client. The wrapper provides the services that the client expected from the component. The client should not use some services via a wrapper and some services directly, since this makes it aware of implementation details that may change.

For each service that the wrapper provides, it can:

- pass the request directly to the wrapped component;
- process the request itself, without assistance from the wrapped component;
- process the request by adding processing of its own, while still using the wrapped component to provide its original processing.

The need to wrap a component often arises as a result of assembly issues and these are covered in the next chapter.

12 Assembling components

Once components have been acquired, harvested from existing applications, or developed from scratch, they are assembled to form at least part of the solution to a particular business requirement.

Assembling a solution may involve:

- building the presentation layer;

- customizing components that offer customization options;

- adding adapters that convert between the interface required by a calling component and the interface offered by the called components;

- resolving mismatches between the functionality of the components to be assembled or the data they store, potentially requiring the wrapping of one or both components.

Building the presentation layer is often part of solution assembly because the front end of an application usually reflects specific user requirements and so is not reusable. However, there may be application components that can be reused in cases where these have been built to go with particular business components, providing standard access mechanisms.

Note that "wrapping" a component, or other code, creates a new component and this activity is therefore component development. Adapters convert between components and sit between them, and their production is therefore part of solution assembly. This separation helps to ensure that components are developed in a way that is context-independent, so that the next attempt to reuse them will not uncover tailorings to the specific context in which they were used that thwart reuse.

However, the need to wrap a component usually arises in the context of the development of a particular solution, and I have therefore chosen to cover in this chapter the assembly issues that give rise to a need to wrap existing code.

12.1   Customizing components

As discussed in the previous chapter, components may be built to offer extension points or customization options that can be used at assembly time. Customization may involve:

- setting parameter values or setting up reference data that the component uses in order to steer its choice of behavior;
- completion of user exits and adding components to satisfy the component's outbound interfaces (i.e. components it uses), maybe including the addition of data access routines that are tailored to the particular environment;
- use of a customization interface to allow controlled customization of a component, e.g. addition of code sections;
- sometimes, recompilation of the component – this is particularly likely to be the case where the component includes code that is used for customization purposes but that should be removed for live running of the component.

12.2   Interfacing with reused components

In this section I outline the main issues that can arise when putting components together – subsequent sections deal with these issues in more detail.

1   It is important to check that each component observes constraints that are required by other components. Observation of constraints must be checked in a variety of circumstances:

- obviously, where one component uses a service offered by another component;
- less obviously, where there is an indirect interdependency between components. For instance, where two components both update the same data, one could potentially create values that the other cannot handle;
- also less obviously, where one component may cause events to occur that should affect another component's processing. In this case, there is a question as to how to ensure that the events will be picked up by the other component. For instance, when a product is withdrawn, outstanding orders for that product are affected. How is the order processing component to be made aware of this situation?

See Section 12.3 on page 150.

2 It may be necessary to introduce "glue" code between components, for instance to convert between one component's view of a service's interface and the other's. This is achieved through the creation of an adapter. See Section 6.3 on page 86.

3 There may be technical issues that mean that adapters must be provided for components so that they can interoperate. For instance, it may be necessary to use an adapter for a component to wrap it as a COM object or to CORBA-enable it.

4 It may be necessary to wrap a component in order to:
- handle data mismatches;
- resolve a functional mismatch, e.g. extend the capabilities of a component;
- ensure that relationships and transactions that cross component boundaries are handled correctly.

Note that, where a component uses the services of another component via a wrapper, *all* services should be invoked via the wrapper. It should not be permissible (because it creates maintenance issues) for a component to invoke some of another component's services via a wrapper and some directly.

Generally, wrapper components should be handled in a separate component development activity, unless the extent of the wrapper is very small.

12.3   Enforcing component constraints

As previously outlined, problems can arise where:

- one component uses another component but has different expectations;
- there is an indirect interdependency between components;
- one component may cause events to occur that should affect another component's processing.

12.3.1   Different expectations

Where you are assembling components, it is important to be able to check the requirements of the two components so that it can be seen whether their expectations are compatible. This process of checking can be greatly assisted by using preconditions and by specifying valid ranges for input and output parameters in the specification of each service. You can then make sure that the client component observes preconditions and that the used component will only supply output values within the ranges accepted by the client component.

Where the two components do have different expectations, you may be able to resolve this by putting intermediate code between the two, using an adapter. The client component would call your intermediate service, which processes input values the used component will not accept, while calling the used component for acceptable values.

The client component should not make assumptions about the result it will get for a given input value. For instance, it should not assume that a debit transaction will be accepted. If it does make such assumptions, this suggests poor component design, which should be corrected where possible.

Inevitably, however, a component makes some assumptions about the type of return results it will receive that may not be valid as the use of a component is extended. For instance, the client component may assume that an account cannot have a negative balance. If you want to use it with a component that allows a negative balance (because the type of account allows it), the client component will require modification or replacement by another component. No use of adapters can resolve this.

12.3.1.1 *Data-related issues*

One component may expect two items of data to be linked, while another does not. If a client component does not provide a component it uses with the information it needs in order to manage a relationship, a data mismatch problem arises. It may be possible to resolve this by using an adapter to place intermediate code between the two components that adds the necessary information.

12.3.2 Indirect interdependencies

Conflicts between components often arise where two components take different views of data. One problem occurs if the component that manages the data is unaware of a relationship that another component expects to exist. This can be handled as described in Section 12.5 on page 157.

If a new component is added that requires new constraints to be observed, it will be necessary to check whether existing components observe these constraints. If an existing component doesn't observe the constraints, the only real options are:

● to relax the constraint in the new component;
● to include code in data access routines that "fixes" the data for the new component, so that it sees what it expects to see;
● to modify the existing component;
● to abandon the idea of using the two components together.

A further option might be to use the database to enforce the integrity constraint, but this helps only if, when the existing component submits data that does not observe the constraint, it can handle the error returned by the database, and if its error reporting is such that the user can understand the problem reported to him or her and resubmit the update in an acceptable form.

To take an example, let us imagine that our existing order entry application makes it possible to enter order items without specifying a valid product code. In a different context, we have decided to use a new order fulfillment component that takes the view that the relationship between order items and products is mandatory.

We could:

- modify the new order fulfillment component to behave benignly if it encounters order items that are not linked with products;
- put a fix in the data access routines for the order fulfillment component which will update the order item, converting the product name into a link with product (assuming of course that this automatic fix is possible);
- change the order entry application so that it does not allow the creation of order items that are not linked with products;
- decide that the new order fulfillment component cannot be used, or that it is time we replaced the order entry application.

12.3.3 Handling events that impact other components

There are cases where events that occur in one component may have implications for other components. For instance, it may be that a decrease in stock levels, managed by one component, should trigger stock reordering in another.

Such cases can often be avoided by designing components such that closely related processing is in the same component. However, event mechanisms provide an alternative approach for dealing with these cases. See the description of event notification in Chapter 5 for an explanation of how this works.

With object technology, or with any technology that supports immediate event notification, a publish/subscribe mechanism can be used to allow other components to be notified of an intended event and to take appropriate action. Alternatively, provided immediate event notification is not needed, a component can post events to a database table, which is read on start-up, or at intervals, by any other component that needs knowledge of the events.

An example of the use of event notification might be to handle the case where a product is discontinued, and an order processing component needs to handle the impact of this on any outstanding orders.

Event notification is also a possible technique for handling the implications for other components of the deletion of a business object in a separate component. (Managing relationships that cross component boundaries is discussed in detail in Section 12.6.)

12.4   Resolving functional and data mismatches

In order to avoid problems when assembling components, it is desirable that components should be developed such that:

- only one business component is responsible for maintaining any particular item of data; (This cannot always apply. Data distribution requirements may mean that the same data must be maintained on multiple platforms.)
- the business logic and the data access logic are separated. This improves maintainability by separation of concerns. It also makes it possible to switch

a business component to use a different data store, isolates the business component from a legacy data structure, and decouples changes to the database structure from changes to the business component;

- checking of data integrity (i.e. maintenance of mandatory relationships, etc.) is placed in the business component (since this is business logic), while any checks that are not part of the business logic, but are required because of the physical implementation, are placed in the data access layer. The user interface will often implicitly enforce data integrity by simply making it impossible to enter data that is not appropriately linked (e.g. making it impossible to create an order that is not linked with a customer), but the user interface should not be the sole location of business logic.

Problems can arise because of:

- redundant logic, with more than one component handling the same business logic;
- data mismatches, where the business component assumes storage of data we are not interested in or we need to store data for which the business component does not cater;
- database mapping, where a component must be adapted to store data in a particular database;
- redundant data, where two components store separate copies of the same data;
- data distribution, where data is to be located at different sites, for instance to provide swift access.

The following sections concentrate on ways of handling these issues that do not involve modifying the components themselves. That is, the discussion is of ways of handling these issues at assembly time, treating the components as black-box. In some cases, modifying the components themselves (if possible) will result in a better solution or will solve a problem that cannot be solved without modification.

12.4.1 Redundancy

Redundancy may be required where processing is distributed. Where feasible, the use of portable code will make it possible to build components for different platforms using the same code base, so avoiding redundancy. If different code is used, inconsistencies are likely to develop and close control must be kept.

Redundancy may also result from the use of legacy applications. The reduction of redundancy that a component-based approach will gradually bring will mean fewer problems resulting from inconsistencies. One approach may be to ensure that redundant code in a legacy application is not used, with the new component being used instead.

12.4.1.1 Multiple components managing the same data

Conflicts between components often arise when there is more than one component managing the same data.

Where more than one component updates the same data, it may be difficult to ensure that all components observe any constraints on how the database is updated. The issues this raises are similar to those discussed in Section 12.3.2 on page 151.

12.4.2 Handling data mismatches

Where there are differences in data formats between two components, we can provide intermediate code to convert data formats, which we place in an adapter component to isolate the two components from it.

Where the component does not manage data that we need, we can wrap the component to add management of the missing data. Section 12.5, on page 157, discusses the particular issues associated with managing missing relationships.

Sometimes, existing fields can be subverted in order to meet requirements. For instance, *Notes* fields may be used for additional data that is required, or unused fields with suitable data formats may be used for a different purpose from that which was originally intended. While this may be a valid short-term solution, it does tend to increase the cost of maintenance by increasing the likelihood of error, so that if such a solution is used, a development activity to improve the solution should be added to the organization's overall development program.

Where the component manages data that we do not need, it is important to know:

- Is it optional data that we can simply omit when making updates?
- If it is required, can we add dummy values or is the data used elsewhere, maybe by other applications, in such a way that dummy values will create meaningless results or positive errors?
- If the data is required elsewhere, can we add input of this data here or require it to be entered previously by the user through a separate function?

Ultimately, if the data is required and we cannot provide it, we cannot use the business component for the intended purpose without modifying it.

- If we add meaningless padding data, we should isolate the addition of this data as far as possible from any code that handles meaningful business logic. Comments should be used to ensure that the reason the code is included is very clear. Adding padding data is risky, of course, and generally poor practice. Subsequent maintenance activities or changes may expose the meaningless data, unaware that this was not meant to happen.
- If we decide to provide for input of the data, we should try to do this in a way that distorts the intended shape of the components as little as possible. This generally means isolating the input of the data, e.g. presenting it in a separate part of the user interface. It may also mean using separate component code to manage it, that can be detached when it is no longer needed.

12.4.3   The component to database mapping

If the business component does not come with data access components included, part of the assembly process may involve adding a data access layer that translates between the view of the data in the business component and the actual requirements of the database. (These may differ either because the business component has been bought or because the database incorporates an older view of the data structure than the business components.)

One aspect to consider when adding a data access layer is the desirability of ensuring that components involved in a transaction should use the same database. Sometimes, more than one data access layer is required to make it possible to use the same business component in different contexts, accessing a different database.

An alternative is to include in the data access component conditional logic that selects the relevant database access logic. It is better not to make other components (e.g. the application or business component) control the choice of database, since this creates an interdependency, making the components less context-independent. (One alternative would be to use global data to hold the necessary information, loading it only when the data access components are first used.)

12.4.4   Redundant data

In some cases, we will decide to use two components which each store a copy of the same data. For instance, we might use two packages that each store customer details. If the two packages do not make it possible to attach our own data access layer, we may not be able to adapt the software to use a common database.

There will also be cases where it does not make sense for two applications to use a common database, for instance where the overlap in terms of data is small and maybe the hardware and software environments used are very different. Extracting the common data into a separate database would mean creating nontrivial transactions that update both the common data and the other data. In such cases, we need a strategy for keeping the duplicate data synchronized. Similar issues arise to those described in Section 12.6 on page 167.

Given the difficulties of merging updates, it is best to minimize the extent to which there are overlapping updates, either by making one application's version read-only or by allowing update to each individual item of data only through one application or the other.

Where this is not possible, there are two strategies available:

- production of reports on differences, so that differences can be resolved manually by rekeying data;

- automated propagation of updates.

In either case, one location should be nominated as the master location for updates.

For automated propagation of updates, those made in the secondary location are recorded and applied later to the master record. Updates made to the master records can be transferred at intervals to the secondary location.

The approach to making the update depends on the type of update. There are two significant types:

- updates that replace data values without regard for the previous value, for instance updates to customer address;
- updates that update data values based on the previous data value, for instance, updates to credit available.

Where values are replaced, an update from the secondary location is applied only if it is later than the value already held. Ideally, only changed values will be transferred. This eliminates the case where the telephone number is changed on the master database followed by the address at the secondary location, but the propagation of the update of the address overwrites the change to the telephone number.

Where values are updated cumulatively, the update needs to be applied as an increase or decrease, rather than an overwrite. Of course, this could mean that an update which, at the time it was recorded, was not thought to cause a credit limit to be exceeded, does in fact do so when it is propagated. The business logic must be built to allow for the implications of this.

12.4.5 Duplicate records

Where records can be created by two different components, it is necessary to find a manual or automatic way of determining whether two records relate to the same thing, and to allow these two records to be merged. It is often possible to detect automatically that there may be duplication, but it usually requires human intervention.

In some circumstances it may not be appropriate to merge the records. For instance, a set of hospital records that were taken without knowledge of another set of records for the same patient should probably not be merged.

It will sometimes be desirable to provide users with a way of either linking or merging duplicates, either through a data conversion process or as part of normal operation of the application.

12.4.6 Data distribution

Data distribution issues are unaffected by the use of components. Data distribution requirements may result in a need for reuse of a component on more than one platform, or for variants of a component that are tailored to the requirements of a particular platform (e.g. allow update of a subset of customer data only).

Data distribution decisions are likely to be based on:

- where data is updated – it is best if all data that is updated together is placed at the same location;

- where data is read – where data is infrequently updated but is frequently read on a different platform, data replication may provide a solution. Data can be updated daily or more frequently, maybe on logon. Code tables are often good candidates for replication.

Data of the same type can be fragmented where access is required from different locations:

- horizontally, by storing subsets of objects of one type at different locations (e.g. store customer details at the customer's local branch);
- vertically, by storing different parts of the same object at different locations.

Fragmentation should normally be carried out so that any updates affect only a single location.

It can be useful to provide snapshot databases, where *ad hoc* query capabilities are required on a workstation, but data does not have to be fully up to date. Similarly summary tables, which summarize information from different locations, can be useful in some circumstances.

12.5   Managing relationships between components

This section discusses strategies for managing relationships between business objects where the related business objects are in different components. A strategy is needed for managing relationships between components even where all data is stored in a single database. This is because we want components to be separable from each other and capable of being used in multiple contexts.

As an example of why relationships are an issue, let us consider an investment account. We could use a business component containing this object in both a pensions application and a banking application. But if we use *Investment Account* in a pensions application, we wouldn't want it to drag with it all the relationships it has with banking-specific business objects, or vice versa. This is why we need strategies to make it possible to maintain the independence of components even where the business objects they contain have relationships that cross the component boundary.

Figure 12.1 illustrates the techniques that are discussed in this section. Note that the terminology used is explained later during the course of the discussion.

12.5.1   Types of relationship maintained across component boundaries

There should be as few relationships between business objects in different components as possible.

If two business objects are highly dependent on each other, to such an extent that they are not separable, they should be put into the same component. This is the case where there is a relationship that is mandatory at both ends. There

Figure 12.1

Techniques for managing relationships

Mapping technique	"Owned" relationships	"External" relationships
Direct link	✓	✓ with mapping table
Proxy: role object	✓ in owning component	✓ in coordinating component
Proxy: application integration	✓ in wrapper of used component	✓ in wrappers of used components

may also be a very close relationship between two business objects that are linked by an optional relationship.[1]

Furthermore, it only makes sense to put related business objects in different components where there is potential for reusing one business object in a context in which the other is not required.

Where there are relationships between objects in different components, we can usefully classify these as:

● "owned"

● "external".

12.5.1.1 "Owned" relationships

With "owned" relationships, business objects of one type establish a relationship with business objects of a second type. The business objects of the first type can be said to "own" the relationship. No transactions directly controlled by the business component containing the second type of business object require knowledge of objects of the first type.[2]

For an "owned" relationship, the component containing the "owning" business object can manage the relationship.

An "owned" relationship is uni-directional (i.e. traversed in one direction only). It creates a one-way dependency between business components. The "owning" business component requires the presence of the used business component. Only the used business component is context-independent and can be used without the owning component (see Figure 12.2).

"Owned" relationships may be:

● mandatory – in this case, the "owning" business objects require the related objects in order to exist;

---

1. Often, such relationships are really internal to a business object, e.g. optional notes that can be attached to some objects.
2. Management reports may navigate from objects of the second type to objects of the first type, but we disregard this since such reports can potentially navigate data in any direction.

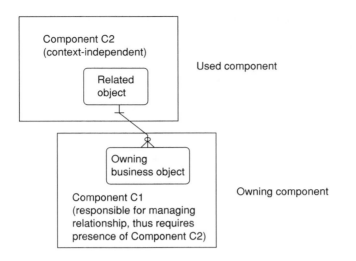

Figure 12.2
Components with
"owned" relationship

- optional – in this case, the relationship is optional at both ends and the relationship is always established by processing that is in the context of the "owning" business object.

12.5.1.2 "External" relationships

With "external" relationships, the relationship is optional at both ends and is not required for any transactions within the direct control of either business component (Figure 12.3).

An "external" relationship is always needed where some transactions navigate the relationship from one end and other transactions navigate it from the other

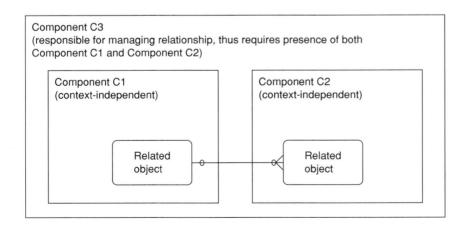

Figure 12.3
Components with
"external" relationship

end, since otherwise the two components become interdependent and cannot be used independently of one another.[3]

An "external" relationship is always required where both components will sometimes be used without the other component being present.

For an "external" relationship, neither of the components that contain the business object will manage the relationship. It will be managed by a further component that requires the presence of both the other components. This component is not artificially introduced but is the logical home for the business logic that manages the relationship, as defined in the component blueprint.

While Figures 12.2 and 12.3 show a one-to-many relationship, the relationships could also be one-to-one or many-to-many in either case.

12.5.2 Representing the relationship

The options for representing these relationships do not generally depend on whether the relationship is "owned" or "external". Possible design options are:

- direct link – in this case, the component that manages the relationship simply stores a direct reference to the related business object, in the form of its primary key;

- proxy – in this case, the managing component includes and stores a representation of the related business object.

To illustrate these options, consider a requirement to develop an order processing application that will use an existing *Product* business component. Figure 12.4 illustrates both the data model of the new *Order Processing* application and a data model of the existing *Product* component. (The *Product* component has been cut out of an existing legacy application. This is why it includes *Catalogs* and catalog-specific *Product Descriptions* that are not required in all contexts in which we use *Product*.)

12.5.2.1 Direct link

Direct links are the simplest way of handling a relationship. They are what we are used to using. Unless there is some specific reason for not using them, they are the obvious choice.

Figure 12.5 shows the result of using a direct link, where the *Order Processing* component "owns" the relationship with *Product*.

Figure 12.6 shows the use of direct links for an "external" relationship. In this case we must add a mapping table that can hold the pair of corresponding primary key values.

---

3. We assume here, of course, that the reasoning behind the component split was sound, i.e. that there is a real possibility of the two components being used independently of one another. If this is not the case, then the two objects should be put in the same component.

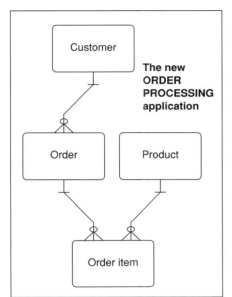

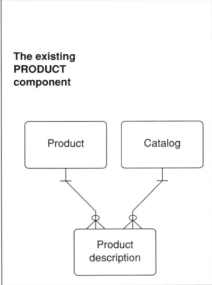

Figure 12.4
A new order
processing application

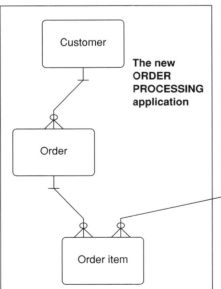

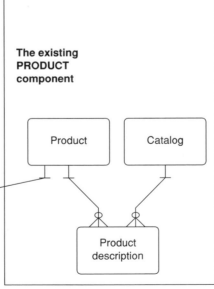

Figure 12.5
Using a direct link for
an "owned"
relationship

Figure 12.6

Using a direct link for an "external" relationship

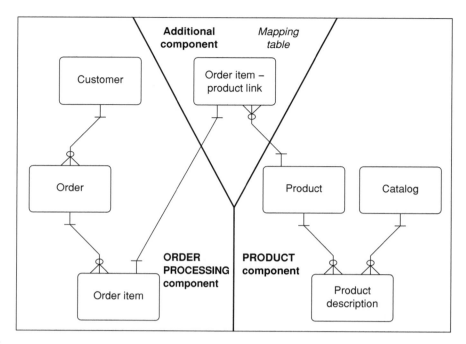

In the case of the *Order Processing* example, an "owned" relationship is more natural than an "external" relationship. It is difficult to imagine a situation in which the *Order Processing* component could be used without the *Product* component also being present. Surely it is really of the nature of an *Order Item* to relate to some item or product that is to be ordered? Wouldn't it be a strange sort of an *Order Item* that did not order anything?

For this reason, the use of an "external" relationship here is unnecessary. However, there are many cases where it will be useful in enabling two components that are otherwise separable to be used independently.

12.5.2.2 Proxies

A proxy represents a business object in one component in the case in which the business object is owned by another component. It makes it possible for the master business object to exist independently of the proxy. The master business object is the one that definitively represents the object – it is the master for synchronization purposes.

A proxy differs from a direct link in that it is a representation of the business object that is capable of maintaining data and that can have behavior. There are two main reasons for using proxy objects as opposed to a direct link.

"Role" objects

A proxy can be a "role" object that contains attributes and behavior that are specific to the use of the master object in a specific context. For instance, the

Customer business object in the *Order Processing* component might be a "role" object that is linked with a Party object in a separate component.

Application integration

Application integration or distribution requirements can also make the use of a proxy desirable. Proxies can be needed if the master business object is not on the same physical database and maybe not at the same physical location as the proxy. Attributes and behavior from the master object are duplicated in the proxy to allow transactions to be carried out at a single location.

In this case, the proxy belongs in a wrapper component that wraps the component containing the master business object. It does not belong in the same component as the related object.

This may not seem obvious at first sight. We assume that the two components are separate for good reasons and that, therefore, the component boundary and the independence of the components should be preserved. If the master business object does not belong in the component containing the related object, its proxy evidently does not belong there either. I will revisit this point following an example of the use of proxies for the order processing case.

Figure 12.7 shows an example where we have decided that product discounts are relevant only in the context of order processing and so have placed these in the *Order Processing* component, creating a proxy for *Product* that represents a "role" object. (In this case, the creation of a proxy may give us more work than benefits in return, since the amount of logic associated with the "role" is small.)

Note that if we were introducing the proxy for application integration reasons, not because we have a use for a "role" object, we would do better to keep

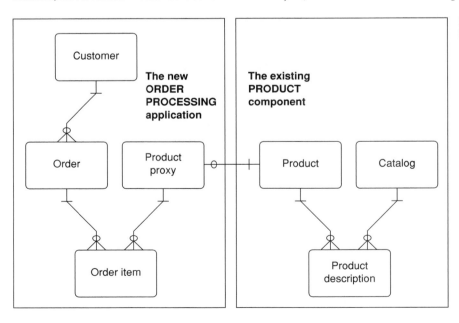

Figure 12.7
Using proxies

it out of the *Order Processing* component. Otherwise, we would have built into the *Order Processing* component implementation-specific assumptions about the context it will be used in. This would hinder reuse, since we might not need the proxy in other contexts in which we use the *Order Processing* component. A change that brings the *Product* component onto the same platform as the *Order Processing* component would also mean that the *Order Processing* component would have to be changed, instead of simply removing the wrapper.

Moreover, we would have breached encapsulation by building knowledge of products into the *Order Processing* component. A single breach of encapsulation dramatically increases maintenance effort, since we can no longer rely on encapsulation being observed in any part of the design. We have to assume that what developers have done in one place they may have done elsewhere as well. We would no longer be able to assume that components that use a *Product* component do not include processing that should only be in the *Product* component. Instead, whenever we made a change of any sort to *Product*, we would have to look into every component that uses it to check that it does not also incorporate this processing.

12.5.3 Identifying the related object

When linking business objects in different components, the foreign key you use could be either a meaningful key or an artificial key or object identifier. Each approach has advantages and disadvantages, and unfortunately it is not possible to make a single recommendation.

12.5.3.1 *Business identifier*

If you use a key that is meaningful in the business world, problems arise if the key values can be updated. If updates are possible, then similar referential integrity issues arise to those involved if the related object is deleted. These are discussed below in Section 12.5.4.

12.5.3.2 *Artificial key*

If you use an artificial key that is not presented on the user interface, two problems arise.

1 There is an implementation-level dependency between the two components. If you swap the *Product* component for another one, or use different *Product* components in different circumstances, the artificial key is likely to be meaningless in the new context, whereas a meaningful key is more likely to be supported.

2 A further data access is required to obtain meaningful values that can be displayed on the user interface (although this may be necessary anyway if the foreign key used is, for instance, a product code).

A form of this problem often arises when previously separate applications are integrated. One application may use social security numbers to identify individuals, while other applications each allocate their own different code. These may be artificial keys that are required by business users to allow swift access to information. Translation between different identifiers becomes necessary when these applications are integrated.

The use of such identification codes is often valuable from the business point of view, although alternatives such as swifter retrieval by more meaningful data (e.g. name and postcode) can reduce the extent to which the business requires codes. Where the organization has multiple identifiers, it is desirable to select a single one on which to standardize over time.

Knowledge that a relationship has two identifiers should reside only on one side of the component boundary. Translation between the two identifiers should happen in only one place. The choice of location for this knowledge may vary. If the existence of multiple identifiers is regarded as a permanent feature of the situation, it makes sense for the component containing the business object to contain this knowledge. Otherwise it may be possible to isolate it within an adapter component.

12.5.4 Managing deletion of the related object

Where a business object within a component has relationships of which the component has no knowledge, deletion of the object raises referential integrity issues. How are we to handle the impact of object deletion on related objects when the component that is deleting the object is unaware that it has these relationships?

There are three standard options for handling the effect of deletion on related objects, and these apply whether components are used or not:

- the relationship is removed (nullified) – this is not a valid option if the relationship is mandatory;
- the deletion cascades to the related object – this means that the related object is also deleted;
- the deletion is prevented from occurring (is restricted) if there is a related object.

The appropriate handling should normally be specified as part of the specification of each relationship.

The simplest way of dealing with referential integrity issues is to avoid them. This can be achieved in different ways.

- Disallowing deletion of objects. Objects are often created by mistake, so if this option is used, it is best to allow deletion until the object's status is changed to one that indicates it has been approved (and for other components not to establish relationships with an object that has not been approved).
- Giving objects a validity period. Objects are never deleted, but their validity may expire. An object that is no longer valid may still be associated with other

objects. For instance, a discontinued product may remain associated with order items. This approach is often appropriate for standing data.

Use of these mechanisms means building into the component an awareness that it has, or may have, relationships that are not under its control, since this is why these mechanisms are needed. On the other hand, the mechanisms do not create any specific dependencies on other components. The component can still be used in different contexts.

A more complicated mechanism for handling deletion is to register relationships. A single generic table could be used for all types of objects that records relationships between objects in different components. Before a deletion request is accepted, the table is checked and the deletion request is rejected if the object has any relationships.

It may be possible to exclude some relationships from this table.

- If the relationship should be nullified on deletion, the component that manages the relationship can do this when the relationship is next accessed, and the related object not found. These relationships can therefore be excluded from the table.

- If the deletion should cascade, it could be argued that this could also be handled later. However, this is risky and I do not recommend it since the second object may itself have relationships that mean that it cannot be deleted. Normally an attempt to delete an object should not succeed if any cascading deletion fails.

With object technology, or with any technology that supports immediate event notification, a publish/subscribe mechanism provides an alternative to the above approaches, allowing other components to be notified of an intended deletion and to take appropriate action. (See Section 12.3.3 on page 152, and the description of event notification in Section 5.4.4 on page 68.)

12.5.5   Bidirectional navigation

The solutions I have described so far are important in maintaining the context-independence of components, so that they can be reused. But sometimes we want to navigate relationships in either direction, without constraint. This is useful for:

- management reporting purposes;
- a flexible user interface that allows you to navigate from any object to any related object.

How can we achieve this without compromising the context-independence of the components?

Actually, we can always navigate from both ends of the relationship provided we build this capability into our components. For an "external" relationship, the managing component can provide services allowing *Products* to be retrieved that are associated with *Order Items*, or *Order Items* that are associated with *Products*.

For an "owned" relationship, the owning component (the *Order Processing* component) can provide these two services.

However, if we want a *generic* solution, the answer is to use a framework. We can build standard logic to handle the navigation of relationships in either direction and remove this from the components themselves, thus protecting their context-independence. It can be made to appear as if *Product* does know about *Orders*, even though in fact there is no code in the *Product* component that makes it dependent on the presence of an *Order Processing* component.

12.6   Managing transactions that cross component boundaries

Where all the business components store their data in the same database, in the same location, transactions that cross component boundaries present few problems. Such a transaction can be handled as follows.

1   The new transaction can be defined as a service that is offered by a business component.

2   The new service may be offered either by one of the business components that manages the data involved in the transaction or by a new business component. The choice depends on where the service logically belongs.

3   Ideally, the new service will not include start transaction or commit statements. These are best handled by the component execution environment, so that the new service itself can potentially be included in another, larger, transaction at some future point in time. If the component execution environment offers no assistance here, a decision must be made either to include the start transaction and commit statements in the transaction, or to make this the responsibility of a separate, workflow-oriented component.

There may be cases where it is tempting to make a presentation component put together a transaction that groups a number of logical transactions. This may be the case where there seem to be application-specific reasons why the new transaction is required, rather than a requirement for a new (reusable) business service. It is argued that no additional logic is required for the bigger transaction – it will simply act as an umbrella pasting the smaller transactions together. Generally, though, this type of argument does not hold water. If there is a reason why a set of updates should be committed as a single transaction, there is usually a new business service, which should be offered by a business component.

12.6.1   Location of control

One case where it is sometimes argued that an application component should be responsible for the overall control of a transaction is where the different transactions involve data access via several processors. At this point, the idea of pushing the control of the transaction to the processor that handles the presentation logic may seem attractive – and the reasoning then suggests that this logic is put in an application component rather than the business component that is, in my opinion, its logical home.

It is desirable that there should be a single point of control that contains the coordination logic. Assuming a two-tier physical architecture, this coordination logic could be placed on the same processor as one of the data access components. The technology used may dictate in favor of this approach.

It is true that the status of the transaction will usually have to be communicated to the application component anyway, maybe suggesting an approach in which the application component and business component are co-located and the coordination logic is on the same processor as the application component.

With a three-tier physical architecture, the middle tier is the most logical place for coordination logic.

12.6.2 Design options for non-trivial transactions

Where a technological solution is not available, it is still possible to produce solutions for some types of non-trivial transaction that span components. However, the component that coordinates the transaction has to be built with the specific environmental constraints in mind, so that switching it to use other components will involve code change.

Note that we are generally forced down this route by existing legacy applications on incompatible technologies, or by genuine requirements for distributed processing. The component-based architecture, toward which we are gradually moving, should use compatible technologies for transactions that cross component boundaries, thus reducing requirements for such workarounds.

Managing the ramifications of two-phase commit yourself is not trivial. If one update transaction commits and the other does not, you can either:

- undo the first transaction, but beware the effects of intervening updates!
- persist with the second transaction until it succeeds (possible if the transaction can only fail for technical reasons, such as non-availability of the relevant computer, not for business reasons that cause the update to be rejected).

The undo transaction could itself fail, resulting in a need either for manual intervention or for a logging mechanism that the application can use to enable it to retry until success is achieved.

I am not attempting an exhaustive coverage of options here. Instead, I will try to highlight some of the issues and some of the alternatives.

12.6.2.1 Update transactions involving enquiries

A transaction that involves enquiries on diverse databases but only updates one database does not normally present problems, unless there are pressing reasons why the data values enquired on must be consistent with one another, or must be known to apply at the exact time at which the update is committed.

Replication of data can provide an alternative to this sort of distributed transaction, particularly where data values do not change often. For instance, details of products could be replicated (if changed) once a day, or on logon, from their master source to the platform on which order processing is carried out.

12.6.2.2   User-controlled transactions

One option is to make the user handle each transaction separately. Suppose we are putting together an existing order processing component and an existing stock allocation component. When an order is placed, we really want stock to be allocated in a single transaction.

Instead of this, we could produce a solution in which the user has to carry out two separate actions:

- place the order
- allocate the stock.

We might be able to add to the stock allocation transaction an update that records the identity of the order for which stock has been allocated. (This update would be put on the same database platform as the stock data.) This makes it possible to find orders for which stock has not been allocated.

While we may want to replace such user-controlled transactions over time, user-controlled transactions can be a viable, pragmatic solution when integrating applications.

12.6.2.3   Sequencing of multiple update transactions

Where we build a larger transaction from existing transactions, each of which is committed independently, the question of undo logic arises. What happens if one transaction successfully commits but the next fails for some reason? Maybe the relevant computer is not online, or maybe the transaction fails some validation checks.

In this case, it is best to put first the transaction that is easiest to undo. For instance, an undo transaction for placing an order might simply involve deleting the order. Where one of the components involved in the larger transaction cannot be modified, but another can, the logical transaction to undo is the one that is carried out by the component that can be modified.

For instance, suppose we have a non-modifiable component that handles order entry. For our application, we have a requirement that, for telephone orders, notes must be recorded of the conversation with the customer during which the order is taken. We need to augment the order entry transaction with a record of this additional information.

We add a coordinating component to manage the new transaction. Since the order entry component is not available for change, whereas the new notes transaction will be newly coded, you provide an undo transaction for the new transaction. The coordinating component first invokes the new transaction, then the order entry transaction. If the order entry transaction fails, then the undo transaction for the new transaction is invoked.

12.6.2.4 Logging the progress of the transaction

Let us consider again the order placement and stock allocation transaction in which we want stock to be allocated when an order is placed. Let us assume that the order processing component is at one location and the stock allocation component at another.

One way to handle the transaction would be as follows.

1 The order processing component (or a coordinating component) stores both the order and a stock allocation request, which is given the status "not complete". (Requests could be stored in a separate table.)

2 The stock allocation component is asked to allocate stock. It may succeed or fail. In the same transaction as the stock allocation, it records the fact that it has been asked to allocate stock for this order.

3 The order processing component is notified of successful completion (in the case of success) and updates its request as successfully processed.

4 On start-up, the order processing component checks for any stock allocation requests which have the status "not complete" and re-actions them.

5 The stock allocation component responds to any stock allocation request by first checking whether the request has already been actioned. It takes the action (if necessary) and anyway confirms that the request has been actioned.

The key to the success of this mechanism is that the logging of the status of the transaction occurs within the same database transaction as the transaction itself. It therefore safely records the current status.

This basic approach can be applied in combination with a variety of approaches to handling the communications between the two distributed components.

● The update request to the stock allocation component could be actioned immediately (although the logic we described makes it unnecessary to wait for confirmation of success).

● The update request could be queued and the processing handled via a store-and-forward mechanism.

● Batch files could be used as another way of queuing updates.

Testing, certification, and maintaining a component catalog

13

This chapter outlines issues relating to the management and maintenance of a portfolio of components. How can their quality be assured, and how can they be made available for reuse or sale?

13.1 Creating regression test packs

A component is intended to be capable of being used in multiple contexts. Before it is accepted in a new context, it is useful to be able to determine whether it functions according to its specification. A regression test pack for a component makes this possible.

Regression test packs are helpful in making it possible to determine whether any unexpected behavior of the component in its new environment is due to the way it is being used or results instead from an error in the component. They also help gain users' trust of a component when a new version is produced.

Regression test packs can be created to allow regression testing of individual components or groups of components. The tests included in a test pack can usually be taken from those defined for system or integration test purposes. The objective is to create a set of tests that exercises a component, demonstrating that it provides the functionality advertised for it.

When changes are made to the component, the tests can be rerun to check that it still functions properly, while the main testing effort can be focussed on the actual change that has been made.

A regression test pack should include:

● test plans

● test set-up procedures

● test data.

Where possible, a test harness or test tool should be supplied so that the tests can be carried out easily. It is highly desirable that the checking of results should be automated. Such test harnesses only allow testing of the isolated component, which means that retesting of the component in context is still likely to be needed.

Components that are reused should, of course, be less error-prone than newly developed software.

13.2 Component certification

What is necessary in order to make a component available for reuse or sale? Obviously, enough information must be made available about the component to make it possible to decide whether it will be useful in the context for which it is being evaluated. This can, and should, be information that treats the component as black-box. This type of information can be maintained in a component catalog, as discussed in the next section.

A further item of importance is that it should be possible to evaluate and trust the component's quality. Within an organization, an independent quality assurance group could take on this role. The availability of a regression test pack, as discussed in the previous section, should also help.

One suggestion for ensuring trust in the quality of components to be sold is a process of third-party certification, in which a different organization would test the component and certify it as fit for purpose. However, although this idea has some attractions, it seems unlikely to become very popular in the commercial world. After all, much software is sold with statements of limitation as to the liability of the vendor if the software does not behave as expected. Why should a third party be willing to accept this liability when the vendor won't?

Given this, the most viable approach for components that are to be sold is likely to be to allow trial use of the component so that the potential user can check that it functions adequately. This means that evaluation copies of a component may be required, with licensing mechanisms such that the component stops functioning after a certain period of time or a certain amount of use.

13.3 Maintaining a component catalog

As the use of CBD becomes more widespread in a development and operational environment, it becomes vital to have a mechanism in place that ensures that the component assets are managed at the enterprise level. This is to protect the enterprise from damage due to misuse of a component by helping to prevent a component from being misused.

Keeping a component catalog makes it possible to find out:

- what components are available;
- the status of these components – planned, under development, in use, etc.;
- the interfaces each component offers and prerequisites for its use;
- who has an interest in the components;
- the importance of the components;
- whether the components are safe.

Effective management of the component catalog is important. Without it, there is a strong likelihood that the organization will replace its legacy of uncoordinated and interdependent systems with a similar legacy of components that duplicate functionality and data, and diverge from the original goal of a planned architecture of reusable assets.

13.3.1   Component catalog location

To avoid redundancy, it is best if the catalog can be maintained using the same tool that is used to manage components. If this is not possible (e.g. because components come from a variety of sources), it is worth considering whether details can be automatically extracted from the locations where components are held and consolidated into a single catalog.

13.3.2   Component catalog entries

For each component, a catalog entry should be maintained that includes the type of information that is contained in the component specification, outlined in Section 6.5.3 on page 97. To recap briefly:

- name and brief description;
- provided and required interfaces – if the component assumes the presence of a particular component, or one of a number of alternative components, to supply the required interfaces, these should be identified;
- events published and consumed;
- component characteristics, including information required by the component execution environment;
- additional information as relevant – quality assurance status, test pack, guarantees (e.g. service levels), caveats/limitations, support contacts, component size, environment considerations (e.g. operating system and platform).

A catalog entry should be created as each component is developed. The entry is created by the developer in coordination with the managers of the component catalog and the custodians of the component blueprint. Each such catalog entry should be cross-referenced to the definition of the planned component in the component blueprint.

13.3.3 Component retrieval

The use of naming standards assists component retrieval. Naming standards should include a glossary, which specifies:

● use of standard abbreviations
● use of standard vocabulary
● use of synonyms and homonyms.

It further assists component retrieval if components are categorized, possibly through the use of keywords. Useful categories include:

● business area or domain
● component type
● platform.

13.3.4 Component metrics

Metrics are useful in determining whether the benefits expected from CBD are being achieved and in highlighting problem areas. Aspects to measure include:

● time taken to provide solutions to business requirements
● number of defects
● maintenance costs
● total cost to functionality ratio
● quality
● rates of reuse.

For reuse, the following types could be measured:

● reuse of each component
● reuse achieved by a given project.

Weighting of reuse statistics to allow for the size of a component (number of function points) may prove revealing.

For component quality, it is useful to produce:

● an assessment of adherence to naming and other standards (with automated production where possible);
● an assessment of which components have proved to have the highest reuse value, or value in terms of improved flexibility and low error rates.

These assessments make it possible to identify problem areas. The metrics can also throw light on successes that can be analyzed to enable practices to be improved and attention to be focussed on the areas that yield best results.

A brief case study

Managing chaos with components 14

This chapter provides a brief, fictional case study of the use of CBD in an organization with existing mainframe-based applications that is evolving toward a component-based approach as it introduces call centers and Internet-based systems. The chapter focusses on the overall evolution of the approach, rather than on the details of component definition.

14.1　The company

Limegreen Insurance is a company that handles individual and company insurance. As this market developed, it also started to offer personal pension schemes. Insurance and pensions were traditionally handled by different business units within the organization, with little or no overlap in how they were organized. Each area had its own mainframe system. Back-office staff handled the paperwork, while front-office staff sold policies and handled customer enquiries.

14.2　The challenges

The challenges Limegreen Insurance faced, and still faces, are typical of those addressed by many companies over the past 20 years.

- There have been changes in how products are sold. The company used to have its own salesforce that would visit potential customers in their homes. This mode of selling has decreased in importance dramatically. Most sales are now made via third parties. The company also sees potential in the Internet, and would like to make use of this medium to increase the proportion of direct sales it achieves.

- There has been an increasing trend toward dealing with third-party sales organizations electronically, via Internet-based or other EDI-based systems.

- There has been a move away from communication primarily using letters toward use of the telephone, leading to the introduction of call centers. More recently, e-mail and the Internet have become important communication channels. When using the telephone, customers expect instant response. They also expect Limegreen Insurance to have to hand information about all their dealings with the organization, rather than being asked to communicate separately with each individual part of the organization.

- To keep up with the competition, it has become necessary to launch new products more quickly than was possible previously.

Faced with these challenges, the management, also influenced by changes in business thinking, decided to reorganize the company away from large, vertical splits based on product type toward smaller business units that are oriented toward addressing the needs of certain types of customer. In particular, it was decided that different business units should be set up to handle the needs of different types of customer – one business unit to handle the needs of individual customers, one to handle those of small corporate customers, and one to handle large corporate customers. Each business unit was to be capable of handling all the products relevant to their type of customer. There would be commonality across the business units in that the same business basics apply; however, the processes and workflow required would differ.

To assist in meeting some of these needs, some new systems were developed. For instance, there is now a call center application that deals with sales. This application handles the sales process up to the point at which an application is received. Then the existing mainframe applications come into play. (Incidentally, this gave rise initially to a unity of information issue – a prospect to whom you sell might already be an existing customer, and this might be important during the sales process, but a unified view of information about the customer was not available.)

To address the need to be able to introduce new products effectively, a monolithic package, handling a particular part of the business, was introduced. There was much debate on the wisdom of this, as the package's lack of flexibility was seen as likely to cause problems in the future, but it ultimately had to be accepted as a stopgap solution that enabled some business requirements to be met that could not otherwise be met in the timeframe required for the business to remain competitive.

A problem that remained intractable was the need to refactor the mainframe applications so that they could match the changes in organizational structure and to make it possible to present the unified customer-oriented view that was required. To achieve this, it seemed logical to move away from the monolithic applications of the past toward a more component-based approach. Now all that was needed was to organize for this.

14.3   Organizing the change

There had previously been separate IT departments for the different parts of the organization, with a small unit that was charged with harmonizing practices across the organizations and looking for synergies. This small unit had one of the most frustrating jobs – empowered to advise, but not in a position to achieve anything useful.

Now, with the reorganization of the business as a whole, IT was centralized under a new IT director recruited from outside the organization. At first, the new IT department simply carried on business as usual, leaving people's roles relatively untouched as the new management team got to know each other. A workgroup was set up to carry out a review of the organization's systems as a whole and to recommend how to move forward.

Progress at this point seemed slow.

14.4   The modeling challenge

A group of bright analysts was asked to model the organization's systems and they started by developing a data model. They were left to carry out this activity over an extended period of time while critical issues diverted management's attention to other topics. Over time, they developed a comprehensive model, full of detail.

The problem was to persuade project teams developing new applications to use this model. A feedback process kicked in. According to the project teams, the model was full of detail and overcomplexity that showed a lack of grasp of the realities of application development.

As one example, the model had developed a complex model for business parties and organizations. This included an approach to modeling communication methods that allowed each individual to be associated with addresses, telephone numbers, e-mail addresses, and so on, with the correct communication method being chosen based on the type of communication. An affected project team argued that its application only dealt with customers, not other types of business party, and that the communication method was not variable – communicating with customers was by mail. The central team's data model was unnecessarily complicated. It would never be possible to turn such an overcomplicated model into a physical database design that had any chance of performing efficiently.

The project teams won the battle and proceeded to develop their applications using the data models they chose. While the corporate data model was not wholly useless, the effort to produce applications that incorporated a standard view of data across the organization had not been successful.

14.5   The second wave

As the new business units were set up, it became necessary to reorganize the IT department to reflect the new structure. Given the obvious pain involved in reworking the software to work with the new organizational structure, it was decided that a flexible software structure was high on the list of priorities. Yet again, a component-based approach was proposed as a way of addressing this.

A quick analysis broke down the organization's requirements into a number of key areas, such as policy, product, party (covering all external partners of the organization), investment, and so on. These elements reflected the core business basics – and they mapped to business components. The model seemed, however, too close to the failed central data model initiative. It was decided that the IT organization could not be split around these categories but must clearly reflect the business organization and therefore the application-oriented and workflow-oriented view.

A small group of business architects was created, with each architect responsible for ensuring that the software needs of a particular business unit were met. The business architects were chosen for their analytical skills rather than their technical expertise. They were people with a strong understanding of the business. They were given responsibility for maintaining an overall plan and a long-term view of the capabilities which applications should have. They scoped individual projects, which were then executed by project teams, each with their own application architect, which developed the software itself.

A separate technical architecture group was also set up. This started to define common technical standards and to identify the set of platforms on which the organization should converge over time.

14.6   The component wave

It gradually became clearer how the organization could move toward components. The business architects had become an invaluable part of the organization with in-depth understanding of their particular areas of functional expertise. While some managers argued that every individual should be replaceable, it became obvious that the in-depth understanding that the business architects had acquired was invaluable and required at least an apprenticeship to acquire. It also became apparent that the business architects had formed a common view of what the key components were and that a draft component blueprint could be formalized.

The gaps between this and the applications that the organization possessed were large and painfully obvious.

An approach was decided on in which existing monolithic applications would remain in use, but new requirements would be met by producing new components. Over time, as new components are developed to meet requirements, the bulk of code should shift from monolithic applications to smaller components – where the pragmatic approach of this organization dictates that these components will still be quite large.

The use of components also facilitates the use of alternative presentation methods. The same set of business components can be used, with a different front end, for the Internet-based business and for business conducted via third parties, or via the call center.

A small group was created to be a component management group, charged with defining an approach to specifying components. Their task is not to provide guidelines for selecting the set of services to include in a component but to provide a specification standard. Using this standard, project teams can specify components, which are reviewed both by the business architects to ensure that they meet business requirements, and by the component management group to ensure they conform to standards and do not duplicate other components that have already been created. The component management group's role is low-key in that they can advise and discuss but are not empowered to dictate solutions. Over time, their role has become that of administrators, managing the component catalog. Their low-key role helps the project teams feel that they remain in charge of their destinies and that their contribution is not being devalued.

Organizationally, all has gone surprisingly well. Good (enough) management (for when is management ever good?) has understood that an organization consists of a network of relationships between real people, all with their individual needs, and has navigated through the changes without leaving individuals feeling that their role, or the interesting parts of their role, have been taken away. The wheels of change have moved slowly, but the organization is still small enough for its change to be relatively fast, compared with that of some of the businesses around it.

14.7   The component blueprint

Over time, the blueprint has been refined in each of the individual areas that were originally identified.

In the area of product definition, a particularly bright individual working in one of the business units undertook an analysis of the components of products and the ways in which products vary, resulting in a model for product definition that was intended to make it possible to launch new products rapidly. To enable configurable definition of products, many different processes involved in administering policies were identified, and in particular an analysis of the differences and commonality in those processes was undertaken. As a by-product of this analysis, it became easier to define the components that should be used for policy administration, and to decide how to define variation points in them.

In the area of party management, the introduction of components made it possible to find an alternative solution to the earlier data model clash between the central data modelers and the individual project teams. A *Party* component was developed that handles the aspects of business partners that are common to all types of business partner, including management of addresses. Components that handle individual types of party (e.g. customers) and quite often individual types of customer (e.g. customers of a particular type of product) have also been developed and are used in the individual applications to which they are relevant.

14.8   The technical challenges

The technical challenges remain non-trivial. Limegreen Insurance has converted to OO development over a period of time and now develops for preference in Java.

The first components were developed to use CORBA for communication with presentation servers and MQSeries for communication with existing mainframe applications. Early applications were sometimes flawed by a failure to understand the need to restrict the number of distributed communications, but more experience of distributed application development has led to improvements in this area.

The organization has also started to use EJB for some components, but is still on a steep learning curve. In addition, XML is used increasingly as a way of mapping between applications and components.

Distributed transactions remain a problem that is largely avoided. Transactions across heterogeneous environments remain problematic, and avoidance seems the best approach. Maybe, as more components are built using the same underlying infrastructure, this problem will become less acute.

It is difficult to predict what new technologies may arrive on the scene. One approach might be to standardize on a particular technology, and this is the organization's intention. However, given the possibility that today's standard technology will be tomorrow's legacy, the organization is hoping that a component-based approach, together with the use of flexible interface techniques, will help to provide a level of insurance against change, making it possible to move to new technologies while still being able to leverage the library of existing components.

14.9   Managing software change

As components change to meet new requirements, the question arises, "Should the new component version be rolled out across all applications?" The preferred answer is that a change should be taken at once only by the part of the organization that needs it. If other units use a separate copy of the component, they should upgrade (at the latest) at the time at which they next require changes to the component.

Sometimes, however, this has proved a difficult issue to negotiate with business units insisting on cloning their own variant of a component rather than accepting changes they feel they do not need but would have to test.

14.10   Conclusion

Component use is still in its early stages, although at the time of writing some organizations can claim up to five years' experience with it while the ideas have developed. It is not a panacea for all evils or a magic wand to be waved. Indeed, it should be apparent that many of the problems faced are the same whatever the approach. The relative health of an organization in terms of how it enables its people to contribute, how it looks after their needs, and how it adapts to change are key and elusive factors. Nevertheless, while components are not the be-all and end-all, they do seem to offer a way of thinking about software development that can take us a step forward.

Glossary

Abstract. An abstract service or operation has a defined interface and purpose, but is not implemented and is therefore not executable. Abstract services can be defined for component supertypes. Subtypes of the component implement the abstract service as a concrete service. Similarly, abstract operations are defined for object superclasses and implemented as concrete operations in subclasses of the object class.

Adapter. An adapter converts between the technical requirements of the caller and the technical requirements of the invoked component. An adapter might, for instance, be used between a C++ component and a client component that cannot invoke C++ directly, or it might be used to convert interfaces, set switches, or manage security.

Application. A package of software, sponsored as a whole, that meets an identifiable set of user needs – i.e. delivers a coherent set of use cases to one or more end users.

Application architecture. An application architecture defines the constellation of components used to supply the logic required for a specific application. It defines how the building blocks are put together.

Application component. Application components contain logic from the presentation domain. They manage the user interface (and other interfaces handled by the presentation domain) and interact with business components to provide an application that meets users' requirements.

Application renewal. Application renewal extends the return on investment of existing applications through extension, enhancement, web and e-commerce enablement, application integration, and improvements to software quality and system security.

Architecture. An architecture comprises the set of rules, guidelines, and conventions used to define the structure of a system in terms of its component parts, including how the component parts of that system communicate and interoperate.

Attribute. An attribute is the smallest unit of information that describes a single characteristic of a business object, entity, or relationship. For instance, Customer Name is a likely attribute of a Customer entity.

Black-box. A component is black-box if details of its internals (design or source code) are unavailable and unnecessary in order to use the component.

Business analysis. Business analysis involves building an application-independent representation of a business domain for which applications may be built.

Business component. Business components contain the core business-related logic that falls into the business logic layer. They include workflow (or control) logic, and business objects.

Business domain. An area of the business that can be considered as a subject in its own right, such as accounting, product development, foreign exchange, loans, electronic commerce.

Business logic layer. The business logic layer contains the core business-related logic that represents what the end user would regard as the subject matter of an application. It is responsible for ensuring that business rules are observed, and for maintaining the integrity of corporate business data.

Business model. A business model provides an application-independent representation of the business domain for which applications might be built.

Business object. A business object is any entity that participates in a business process, has a unique identity, and has a life cycle that can be expressed as a series of state changes. Business objects have attributes and also operations that can be carried out on the business object.

Business process. A business process is a collection of activities that takes one or more kinds of input and creates an output that is of value to the customer.

Cardinality. Cardinality defines the maximum and minimum number of business objects or instances of an entity that are related to another business object or instance of an entity.

Cohesion. Cohesion describes the strength of the relationships within a component. Within a component, high cohesion is desirable.

COM. Component Object Model is Microsoft's architecture for component software. COM defines a binary standard for component interoperability within and across process boundaries through interfaces that are independent of implementation languages. Implementations based on COM include Microsoft ActiveX (previously OLE) for component software services, MTS (Microsoft Transaction Server) for transaction services, and OLE DB for data access services.

Component. A component is an independently deliverable unit of software that encapsulates its design and implementation. A component offers services that can be invoked by its clients, thus allowing it to be combined with other components into a larger whole.

Component-based development. The process of building and delivering applications that are built using components through a combination of purchase, reuse, reengineering, and new development of components, followed by their assembly into applications. CBD requires a planned development strategy to ensure that the components used will fit together successfully.

Component blueprint. A component blueprint defines the set of components that meets a business's specific needs.

Component execution environment. A component execution environment provides the supporting runtime environment for a component.

Component model. A component model defines the types of building block, or component, that will be used to build an application, as well as constraints on how components of different types can be connected.

Componentware. Componentware refers to software assets that are useful for CBD, and can be bought and sold.

Concrete. A concrete service or operation is one that is implemented and can be executed (as opposed to an abstract service or operation).

Constraint. A constraint is a rule that controls the values of business objects, attributes, and relationships.

Container. A container is a specific instance of the software (component execution environment) that provides the supporting runtime environment for a component.

CORBA. Common Object Request Broker Architecture is an OMG standard for Object Request Brokers.

Coupling. Coupling describes the strength of the relationships and interdependencies between separate components. Between components, low coupling is desirable.

Data access component. Data access components include logic from the data access layer. They map between the view of the data incorporated in the business logic layer and the actual format in which it is stored, and handle the physical access and update of the data in a way that is specific to the database or flat file system in use.

Data access layer. The data access layer is responsible for storing and retrieving data, typically using a database management system, although flat files can also be used.

Delegation. Delegation is a mechanism whereby a component that is asked to provide a service does so by delegating the request to another component or piece of software. Strictly, delegation involves knowledge on the part of the software (to which the request is delegated) that delegation is involved. Less strictly, delegation does not imply such knowledge on the part of the software to which the request is delegated.

Design pattern. A design pattern explains a general design that addresses a commonly recurring design problem. It describes both the problem and alternative solutions. Solutions are often described in terms of possible standard patterns for the interaction between objects or components. To solve a specific design problem, the pattern is applied to the problem to produce a specific, concrete solution.

Domain. A domain addresses a specific subject matter that can be considered in its own right.

Encapsulation. Encapsulation is any mechanism that hides the implementation of an object or component so that other components do not need to be aware of its internals.

Entity. An entity is something real or abstract about which information is collected. Entities are defined using entity-relationship modeling techniques.

Event. An event is an incident that requires some response. An event happens at a point in time and has no duration. A business event is an event to which the *business* must respond.

Façade. A wrapper component provides a façade through which it is possible to access services that are implemented in the wrapped legacy application or component.

Foreign key. A foreign key is used to associate one entity with another related entity. The foreign key usually consists of the primary key of the related entity.

Framework. A software framework is prefabricated software that provides a partial solution for a family of related problems. A framework predefines the main data and control flow infrastructure. The implementation is usually incomplete and is used, extended, and customized by application builders to deliver a specific solution. With an OO framework, the application builder must often build subclasses to produce a functioning application.

Function point. A measure of expected functionality for a delivered component or application that is based on an algorithm that computes a weighted sum of inputs, outputs, enquiries, master files, and interfaces to other components or applications.

Granularity. Granularity refers to the general size of a set of components. Fine-grained components are small, while coarse-grained ones are large. Function points are more useful for measuring granularity than lines of code, as the number of lines of code required for the same amount of functionality varies depending on the programing language.

IIOP. OMG's Internet Inter-ORB Protocol provides interoperability between CORBA-compliant ORBs. IIOP is the TCP/IP transport mapping of a General Inter-ORB Protocol (GIOP). IIOP enables requests to be sent to networked objects managed by other ORBs in other domains.

Inheritance. A subtype component inherits from its supertype component the behavior (services) defined for the supertype component. Inheritance is a concept taken from OO that is usually applied to objects but can also be applied to components.

Intantiation. An instance is an individual case of an abstraction such as a class of objects or a computer process. To instantiate is to create such an instance by putting it somewhere, for instance in memory.

Interface. A component may have one or more interfaces, where each interface contains one or more services that can be invoked by clients of the component. Each interface groups a set of related services that share some common purpose, such that a user of one service is likely to require the use of other services in the interface.

Introspection. The ability of a component to provide information about itself, e.g. details of its interfaces and the services they contain, and details of parameterization options. Such a capability can be used by a component assembly environment to enable it to provide a developer with intelligent assistance with the task of assembling an application.

Layer. Layers organize software into separate functional components that interact in a sequential and hierarchical way, with each layer usually having an interface only to the layer above it and the layer below it. Communication programs are often layered. The reference model for communication programs, Open System Interconnection (OSI), is a layered set of protocols in which two multilayered programs, one at either end of a communications exchange, use an identical set of layers. The layers defined in this book define the relationships between components that operate at the application level of the OSI model.

Legacy application. A legacy application is an existing application with an architecture that makes it inflexible to meet future requirements for change. While it may originally have been well engineered, its structure and maintainability may have deteriorated as a result of changes applied over the years. In addition, it was not designed for interoperability and is not built from components.

Logical unit of work. A logical unit of work is a set of updates that should either succeed as a unit or fail as a unit. In other words, either all the updates involved in the logical unit of work should be committed to the database, or none of the updates involved should be made. While a transaction usually includes only one logical unit of work, in principle more than one logical unit of work can be combined into a single transaction.

Object. An object is an instance of an object class. It includes operations and the data structure on which the operations operate. It has a state, defined by the values of the data it contains, and is capable of responding to messages using the operations defined for it in the class definition.

OMG. The Object Management Group is a software consortium that produces computer industry specifications for interoperable enterprise applications. Its flagship specification is the multi-platform Model Driven Architecture (MDA). It has also established an architecture (the Object Management Architecture or OMA) and standards for distributed objects, including CORBA.

Operation. An operation is processing that can be requested as a unit from an object. Objects of different classes may be able to perform the same operation. An operation has a signature which consists of the name and argument list for the operation. Operations are implemented as *methods* where there may be more than one implementation (method) for a given operation. While objects offer operations, components offer services. These are parallel concepts with different names to avoid confusion.

ORB. An Object Request Broker enables objects to transparently make requests and receive responses in a distributed heterogeneous environment. An Object Request Broker implements the OMG's CORBA standard.

PDA. Personal digital assistant is used to describe any small mobile hand-held device that provides computing or information storage and retrieval capabilities, for instance for calendars and address book information.

Persistence. Persistence defines how long objects continue to exist – for the duration of the program's execution or longer.

Precondition. A precondition is a condition which must be true if a process (e.g. service or operation) is to work. Before invoking the service or operation, the caller should ensure that the precondition is true. The service or operation may additionally check the precondition and return an error if it is not observed.

Presentation layer. The presentation layer handles the interfaces between the application and the external world in the form of users and other external interfaces (e.g. other systems). It converts between the presentation formats required externally and the format in which requests should be made to the components in the business logic layer.

Primary key. A primary key consists of one or more attributes (maybe including foreign keys) that uniquely identify an object or an instance of an entity. For example, Employee Number might be the primary key of an Employee entity or object.

Referential integrity. Referential integrity rules define what should happen to related business objects or entities when a business object or relationship is deleted, or a business object's primary key is updated.

Reflection. Reflection in Java allows an executing Java program to examine or "introspect" itself, allowing the dynamic retrieval of information about classes, methods, and data structures.

Relationship. Relationships link two business objects or entities. They represent business rules that govern associations between business objects. In general, relationships between business objects are relatively static and do not change frequently. Relationships have a defined cardinality and are labeled with role names that describe the role each business object plays with respect to the other.

Role object. A role object is used in one business component to represent a role that a business object plays in a particular context. The core part of the business object is often contained in a separate business component.

Service. A service is a function or procedure that is offered for use by a component. To invoke a service, the client specifies the service name and provides input arguments. On completion, the service returns output arguments. While components offer services, objects offer operations.

Software infrastructure. A software infrastructure is used to incorporate those parts of an application that can be standardized. It may include user interface and data access elements, as well as other aspects (e.g. security). Often, the aspects included in the software infrastructure can be provided as a prebuilt component framework, together possibly with code generators, that can be used for multiple applications.

State. A state represents a condition a business object may be in during which it behaves in a given way. The state is determined by the values of the attributes and relationships of the business object. When certain events occur, the state of the business object changes.

Subtype. A subtype defines a subset of objects belonging to a supertype. For instance, if Animal is a supertype, then Monkey is a subtype. Any object (business object, component, entity, event, etc.) belonging to a subtype incorporates (or inherits) the characteristics of its supertype and adds characteristics, e.g. behavior that is specific to the subtype.

Supertype. A supertype defines common characteristics that are inherited by objects belonging to its subtypes.

Technical architecture. A technical architecture prescribes the technical environment (the technologies to be used) and the software infrastructure.

Template service. Template services implement processing only by invoking abstract operations that the component does not implement. These abstract operations must be implemented in a component that inherits from the component.

Tier. The parts of a software application can be distributed between several tiers, each located on a separate computer in a network.

Transaction. A transaction is a logical unit of work. It is a unit that will be committed to the database as a single unit, or rolled back. From the point of view of the user, transactions are atomic.

Use case. A sequence of interactions initiated by an actor (a user or external system in a given role) in dialog with the system yielding a result of measurable value to that actor.

User task. A user task describes how a single user (which may be another system) uses the application to handle a single external event or time trigger, taking one significant input and dealing with it fully. It usually involves the user selecting an entry in a menu of user tasks, and may involve a number of transactions. It may be suspended and completed on another occasion, but can be (and usually is) completed at one sitting. User tasks are the items that can be put together in workflows.

Web service. Web services allow applications to communicate and share data over the Internet, regardless of operating system, device or programing language.

White-box. A white-box component or application is one for which the design and source code is made available. The component or application can be modified by changing its source code.

Workflow. Workflow relates to the tracking and managing of work in a team environment. Workflow is a manual or automated approach for routing this work from one individual or group to another. The "content" of the workflow is the description of the movement of information, products, material, and the sequence of activities in response to a business (physical) event.

Wrapper component. Wrapper components are application, business, or data access components that have (externally) a shape and scope that is in line with the planned application architecture. Internally, they provide the planned services by encapsulating another piece of software which does not have the required form – either a part of a legacy application or a component that requires enhancement. The internal structure of the wrapper component is not visible to the user of the component.

References

Allen, P. (2000) *Realizing e-Business with Components*, Addison-Wesley, New York.

Booch, G. (1994) *Object-Oriented Analysis and Design with Applications*, 2nd ed., Benjamin/Cummings, Redwood City, California.

Cheesman, J. and Daniels, J. (2000) *UML Components*, Addison-Wesley, Boston, Massachusetts.

D'Souza, D. and Wills, A. (1999) *Objects, Components and Frameworks with UML*, Addison-Wesley, Reading, Massachusetts.

Fowler, M. (1997) *Analysis Patterns: Reusable Object Models*, Addison-Wesley, Menlo Park, California.

Fowler, M. (1997) *UML Distilled: Applying the Standard Object Modeling Language*, Addison-Wesley, Reading, Massachusetts.

Gamma, E., Helm, R., Johnson, R. and Vlissides, J. (1995) *Design Patterns: Elements of Reusable Object-Oriented Software*, Addison-Wesley, Reading, Massachusetts.

Goldberg, A. and Rubin, K.S. (1995) *Succeeding with Objects: Decision Frameworks for Project Management*, Addison-Wesley, Reading, Massachusetts.

Herzum, P. and Sims, O. (2000) *Business Component Factory*, Wiley, New York.

Jacobson, I., Christerson, M., Jonsson, P. and Övergaard, G. (1992) *Object-Oriented Software Engineering: A Use Case Driven Approach*, ACM Press, Addison-Wesley, Reading, Massachusetts.

Kassem, N. and the Enterprise Team (2000) *Designing Enterprise Applications: with the Java™ 2 Platform, Enterprise Edition*, Sun Microsystems, June.

Rumbaugh, J., Blaha, M., Premerlani, W., Eddy, F. and Lorensen, W. (1991) *Object-Oriented Modeling and Design*, Prentice-Hall, Englewood Cliffs, New Jersey.

Sims, O. (1994) *Business Objects: Delivering Cooperative Objects for Client-Server*, McGraw-Hill, London.

Szyperski, C. (1997) *Component Software: Beyond Object-Oriented Programming*, Addison-Wesley, New York.

Taylor, D. (1990) *Object-Oriented Technology: A Manager's Guide*, Addison-Wesley, Reading, Massachusetts.

Wirfs-Brock, R., Wilkerson, B. and Wiener, L. (1990) *Designing Object-Oriented Software*, Prentice-Hall, Englewood Cliffs, New Jersey.

Yourdon, E., Whitehead, K., Thomann, J., Oppel, K. and Nevermann, P. (1995) *Mainstream Objects: An Analysis and Design Approach for Business*, Yourdon Press, Prentice-Hall, Upper Saddle River, New Jersey.

Index

Also in the Object Technology Series

UML and the Unified Process
Jim Arlow and Ila Neustadt

This book provides an indispensable guide to the complex process of object-oriented analysis and design using the Unified Modeling Language (UML). It describes how the process of OO analysis and design fits into the software development lifecycle, as defined by the Unified Process (UP).

UML and the Unified Process contains a wealth of practical and useful techniques that can be applied immediately. You will learn OO analysis and design

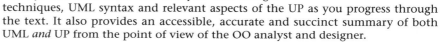

techniques, UML syntax and relevant aspects of the UP as you progress through the text. It also provides an accessible, accurate and succinct summary of both UML *and* UP from the point of view of the OO analyst and designer.

This book provides:

- Chapter roadmaps, detailed diagrams and margin notes allowing a rapid overview, enabling you to focus on your needs
- Outline summaries for each chapter making it ideal for revision and a comprehensive index, so the book can be used as a reference

*The accompanying website (***www.umlandtheunifiedprocess.com***) provides:*

- A complete worked example of a simple e-commerce system
- Useful links to Open Source and proprietary software

ISBN 0 201 77060 1

Visit us on the world wide web at
www.it-minds.com
www.aw.com/cseng

Find more information about the **Object Technology Series** at
www.aw.com/cseng/otseries

From the Component Software Series

Realizing eBusiness with Components
Paul Allen

Unfortunately, there is a great deal of hype and over-expectation surrounding e-business. Many organizations are jumping on the e-business bandwagon without understanding what they are getting into. Lack of planning and analysis, resulting in inflexible solutions that are unable to integrate with existing systems, are all too common. At the same time, e-business calls for a closer relationship between those involved in business development and those required to support these initiatives within the company's information technology infrastructure.

This book is designed to provide practical advice for planning, analysis and design of e-business systems using component-based development (CBD). Just as e-business is more than a series of web pages, so CBD is not just an approach to problem-solving using software building blocks. It includes architectures, processes, modeling techniques, economic models and organizational guidelines, all of which are well placed to ease migration of large organizations to e-business.

The author defines the key concepts relating to CBD, and introduces component standards, component frameworks, middleware and all the relevant internet technologies. The book also deals with issues such as the business case for adopting CBD, pragmatic approaches to modeling business requirements, putting CBD to work using the Catalysis process, migrating to CBD from legacy systems, and the issues associated with sourcing components from off-the-shelf purchasing to bespoke design.

This book shows you:

- how to obtain commitment for a CBD strategy at board level
- how to deploy catalysis modeling techniques and other commercial approaches
- how to use component modeling techniques to create innovative eBusiness solutions
- how to gain competitive advantage with TNBT and Collaborative Commerce

The core of the book is an extensive example that tracks the experiences of a typical company, with a traditional set of business processes and supporting software systems, through various stages along the road to e-business.

ISBN 0 201 67520 X

Visit us on the world wide web at
www.it-minds.com
www.aw.com/cseng

Find more information about the **Component Software Series** at
http://cseng.aw.com/catalog/series/0,3841,1,00.html